JOHN MUIR'S AMERICA

"The mountains are calling me and I must go. . . ."

IMAGES OF AMERICA SERIES

DISTRIBUTED BY

CROWN PUBLISHERS, INC.
NEW YORK

JOHN MUIR'S
AMERICA

Photographs by Dewitt Jones - Text by T. H. Watkins

John Muir's desk in Martinez hcme.

PAGE 1: Jeffrey pine, Yosemite National Park, California.

PAGES 2–3: Glacier Bay National Monument, Alaska.

PAGES 4–5: Petrified Forest National Park, Arizona.

PAGES 6–7: Yosemite Valley at sunrise.

Library of Congress Cataloging in Publication Data

Jones, Dewitt
John Muir's America.

(Images of America series)
Includes index.
1. Muir, John, 1838–1914. I. Watkins, Tom H.
II. Title.
QH31.M9J66   333.7′2′0924 [B]   75-30536
ISBN 0-517-526387

FIRST EDITION

Table of Contents

Acknowledgments

The authors and publisher wish to thank the following individuals and organizations for their help in the making of this book: Marshall Kuhn, chairman of the Sierra Club's history committee, who not only read the book in manuscript, but was instrumental in bringing writer and photographer together in the first place; bibliographer William F. Kimes, whose encyclopedic knowledge of Muir's life and works, and singularly sharp eye in reading the manuscript, were of immense help; Jack Gyer, curator, Yosemite Archives; Bruce Fincham, valley district interpreter, Yosemite National Park; and Christie Hakim, director of the Sierra Club's William E. Colby Memorial Library. Any errors of fact or interpretation are, of course, the sole responsibility of the authors.

Original drawings by John Muir are from the Yosemite Collection, reproduced here by permission of the National Park Service and the courtesy of the Hanna family. Passages from Muir's unpublished journals are from *John of the Mountains: The Unpublished Journals of John Muir*, edited by Linnie Marsh Wolfe (copyright © 1966 by John Muir Hanna and Ralph Eugene Wolfe; Boston: Houghton Mifflin, 1938), and are used here by permission of the publisher.

SOURCES OF MUIR QUOTATIONS:

Page 1: Unpublished journal, 1873; used as chapter III heading in *John of the Mountains*. Page 25: *The Story of My Boyhood and Youth* (Boston: Houghton Mifflin, 1913), Sierra Edition, page 21. Page 26: *Ibid.*, pages 58–59. Page 31: *My First Summer in the Sierra* (Boston: Houghton Mifflin, 1911), Sierra Edition, page 56. Page 49: *Ibid.*, page 61. Page 53: Unpublished journal, mid-June 1890; *John of the Mountains*, page 308. Page 57: *My First Summer in the Sierra*, page 131. Page 61: Unpublished journal, undated but probably August 31, 1875; *John of the Mountains*, page 222. Page 62: Letter to J. B. McChesney, December 10, 1872; quoted in William F. Badè's *Life and Letters of John Muir* (Boston: Houghton Mifflin, 1924). Page 81: Probably sometime in June 1877; quoted in Linnie Marsh Wolfe's *Son of the Wilderness* (New York: Alfred A. Knopf, 1945). Page 85: Unpublished journal, May 21, 1870; *John of the Mountains*, page 53. Page 88: Unpublished journals; *John of the Mountains*, page 44. Page 90: Unpublished journal, undated but probably October 1871; *John of the Mountains*, pages 82–83. Page 92: Unpublished journal, August 21, 1872; *John of the Mountains*, page 89. Page 137: Unpublished fragments of Alaska journal, July 11–21, 1890; *John of the Mountains*, page 313. Page 141: Unpublished journal, January 16, 1873; *John of the Mountains*, page 111. Page 145: Unpublished journal; *John of the Mountains*, page 439. Page 151: Unpublished journal, undated but probably sometime in 1913; *John of the Mountains*, page 438.

Preface

The writer approaches this life story with caution. There is, above all, the problem of infatuation. As Catherine Drinker Bowen has pointed out, the biographer's relationship to his subject should parallel that of a successful marriage, beginning with some touchstone of passion and moving from that to commitment, shared experience, acceptance, and finally to that quality of understanding which can sometimes be called wisdom. But, even as in marriage, the biographical relationship too often founders on the rock of the passion that began it, never moving out of that "first, fine, careless rapture" into the realm of insight. When that happens, the result is less biography than eulogy and is generally useless to the larger purpose of the craft: like its cousin, history, biography is one of the tools necessary to the maintenance of a civilization (which is nothing more or less than the sum of those who have gone before), and its purpose is to distill the essence of another man's life and time in such a way that it illuminates some part of ourselves and our own time.

The life of John Muir simply compounds the difficulty, for there have been fewer more appealing lives in the American chronicle. One searches through the evidence of his existence a little impatiently, looking for warts large enough to roughen all those smooth edges. The warts are there—but, Lord, how small they appear! Did he abandon his wife and children for extensive sojourns into the wilderness and for long stretches of writing? Yes, but most often at their encouragement, even their insistence. Was he no stranger to whiskey and wine? Yes, but if anyone ever saw him cross the line from conviviality to drunkenness, it has not been recorded. Was he quite as lusty as any healthy Scotsman? Indisputably, but the rumors that surrounded him in his lifetime, particularly when he took on all the machinery of progress in his later years, were never proved any more substantial than swamp fog, and were quite as malodorous. Did he nurse bitterness over the treatment his father gave him as a child? Yes, but few men have had better reason for bitterness— and, what is more, Muir conquered it near the end of his father's life with an exercise in compassion and understanding that would have been beyond the psychic strength of lesser men. Was he tight with a dollar? Yes, but only during his infrequent business dealings, and then well within the rules of the game; beyond providing for his family's needs (and in his lexicon "family" had a way of including every relative by blood or marriage who lay within reach of his hand), he had no pronounced interest in money. Did he make enemies? Yes—most notably Gifford Pinchot, chief of the U.S. Forest Service and an earnest proponent of utilitarian conservation, and James D. Phelan, once mayor of San Francisco and one of the principal advocates for the destruction of the Hetch Hetchy Valley—but a man who gets through life without enemies can scarcely have lived at all, for he will have believed nothing strongly.

There is precious little grist for the debunker's mill in the life of this man, obviously, and that fact has helped to make it virtually impossible for his memorialists to fully escape the obscuring glow of first love. That glow so completely seduced Muir's first biographer, William Frederic Badè, that his two-volume *Life and Letters* (1924) is almost embarrassing in its lack of any critical sense. That same glow haunted Linnie Marsh Wolfe, his last and best major biographer, throughout her *Son of the Wilderness* (1945), and while she struggled valiantly to get out of its range long enough to present a genuinely human portrait, the attempt was not fully successful. Nor can I promise that this book goes much further along the road to objectivity. I'm not even sure that it is possible.

What the writer is left with, then, is a determination to cut through the mist of admiration and affection enough to get as close as possible to the heart of what this man's life can teach us of hope and understanding in a time that too frequently appears to be spinning out of control. "In wildness is the preservation of the world," Henry David Thoreau wrote, and refined that statement by declaring that "a town is saved, not more by the righteous men in it than by the woods and swamps that surround it." Substitute "civilization" for "town" and add prairies and grasslands and forests and deserts and canyons and rivers and mountains to woods and swamps, and we come near to the vision which defined the life of John Muir. Thoreau perceived the value of wilderness; Muir not only perceived it but *experienced* it as no man before or since.

Consider for a moment the sheer number of wild places that Muir came to know as other men know well-loved rooms: most of the unsettled portions of the Wisconsin River valley and much of southeastern Canada; the mountains, woods, and swamps of Kentucky, Tennessee, South Carolina, Georgia, and Florida; the mountains of Cuba and the jungles of Panama; almost everything there was to know in California, from the Anza-Borrego Desert of the south to the redwood forests of the northern coast, from the Santa Lucias of the Coast Range to Mount Lassen and Mount Shasta, the San Joaquin and Sacramento rivers, the Great Valley which they drained, and the delta which their confluence formed, and—above all—that incredible "range of light" called the Sierra Nevada, with all its pockets and peaks of wonder; the petrified forests and desert canyons of Arizona and the biblical wastes of Nevada and Utah; the rain forests of Washington and the splendid upthrust of the Rocky Mountains; the glaciers of Alaska and the bleak, wild whiteness of the Arctic Circle; the "rubbery wilderness" of the Amazon River and the awesome stretch of the Andes; Victoria Falls, the baobab woods, the Libyan Desert, and the headwaters of the Nile River in Africa; the Black Sea and the Caucasus Mountains of Russia, the river valleys of Siberia, the tablelands of Manchuria; the glacial fjords of the Korean coast and the foothills of the Himalayas; China, Japan, Australia, New Zealand, the Philippines . . . in all of these and more he reached out for the wilderness without which his soul would have shriveled and through which his being was enlarged.

And, through him, so have we all been enlarged. His most visible legacy, of course, can be seen and experienced directly in many of those remaining wild places that he knew and loved himself, for it is largely because of his efforts that they are with us today—particularly that magnificent glacial trench called the Yosemite Valley (and never mind what we have done to it since by loving it so much). This is a very real inheritance, one which we are duty bound to pass on to our children, our children's children, their children, and all the generations of children lost in the distances beyond our own mortality. A second tangible legacy is the necessary existence of the Sierra Club, one of the largest (and most litigious) conservation organizations in the world; his energies helped form it and his convictions gave it substance, and without it our world would have been measurably different—and surely diminished.

All that was enough and more than enough—more than most of us will ever bequeath to the future. But Muir gave us something else, too, if we can but learn to use it. He was an advocate—yes, a zealot—and it is necessary for such men to communicate. The medium of communication that Muir chose was the written word. He was not a professional writer in the sense in which Wallace Stegner has described the breed—as "a body that will go on moving a pen after its heart is cut out." In fact, he hated both the mechanics of the process and the inadequacy of the finished product. "Book-making frightens me," he wrote to his friend

Mrs. Ezra S. Carr, "because it demands so much artificialness and retrograding. . . . Moreover, I find that though I have a few thoughts entangled in the fibres of my mind, I possess no words into which I can shape them. You tell me that I must be patient and reach out and grope in lexicon granaries for the words I want. But if some loquacious angel were to touch my lips with literary fire, bestowing every word of Webster, I would scarce thank him for the gift, because most of the words of the English language are made of mud, for muddy purposes. . . ."

He fretted and strained and cursed under the whip of that language "in the manufacture of which so many brains have been broken," but he wrote. The body of literature he left us is not large—a handful of books, most of them largely anthologies of the articles he wrote for such magazines as the *Overland Monthly, Scribner's,* and *The Century,* and some of them edited and assembled by others after his death. Nor can it reasonably be said that it constituted a major step forward in the evolution of American literature—there were those before him, with him, and after him who wrote with a clearer eloquence, a greater sense of craft.

No, it is neither the quantity nor the literary significance of his writings that gives them weight. It is the quality of vision that they represent, a vision so deeply felt, so carefully structured, so firmly based on direct experience, so consistent through most of a lifetime that we can only stand astonished that it not only developed and matured during Muir's time and place but that it survived them. For everything in that vision stood in utter contradiction to the whole thrust of the society in which he spent most of his life.

The men who ruled that society did so with all the go-ahead philosophies of Darwinian capitalism, using up land, resources, and people in the business of forging the raw outlines of an industrial civilization in a once pastoral land called California. They were men like Collis P. Huntington, who spent most of his active life painstakingly structuring the Southern Pacific Railroad into one of the most solidly-entrenched corporate monopolies in American history. Or they were men like San Francisco's William Chapman Ralston—"Billy" Ralston—who devoted his energies and his Bank of California money toward the creation of an industrial Xanadu on a spit of land at the western edge of the continent—and who was ultimately destroyed by the very system he had helped to shape. Such men called themselves realists and did so with pride. Muir knew them, or men like them, and admired many of them (one of his closest friends in his later life was Edward H. Harriman, who acquired the Southern Pacific Railroad after Huntington's death), but he knew that in the eyes of most of them he was the most impractical of dreamers, a vague flower-sniffer and mountain climber, someone whose eccentricities could be tolerated only so long as they did not interfere with the proper march of that realism they called progress.

But it was Muir who was the realist, and men like Huntington and Ralston who were the dreamers. Such men truly believed—deeply and sincerely—that the measure of a man was stacked in greenbacks and that the measure of a civilization could only be discovered in the intensity of its commitment to unrestricted growth. Muir did not denigrate wealth; as a canny and hardworking farmer he had accumulated quite enough to keep himself and his family in genuine comfort, if not luxury. Nor did he deny the visible advantages of technological progress, for as a certified mechanical genius and technological innovator himself, to reject them would have been to deny part of his own being. "I have this one big, well-defined faith for humanity as a workman," he wrote from his Yosemite cabin in 1872, "that the time is coming when every 'article of manufacture' will be as purely a work of God as are these mountains and pine trees and bonnie loving flowers." That faith never really left him, not even near the end when he knew the gall of defeat in the Hetch Hetchy conflict.

Yet Muir believed—knew—that all of this was by no means enough. He knew that a man who embraced himself as a kind of walking god, who believed himself above nature and invulnerable to its rules, was cutting himself off from the source of his greatest potential strength. "I go to the mountains," he said once, "as a particle of dust in the wind." Become a *part* of the world, he believed, and you enlarge yourself. He would have all men do so: "Climb the mountains and get their good tidings. Nature's peace will flow into you as sunshine flows into trees. The winds will blow their own freshness into you, and the storms their energy, while cares will drop off like autumn leaves."

Further, he knew that any civilization so arrogant as not only to ignore the land which sustained it but also to attempt to destroy it was trifling with social death: "The world, we are told, was made especially for man—a presumption not supported by all the facts. A numerous class of men are painfully astonished whenever they find anything, living or dead, in all God's universe, which they cannot eat or render in some way what they call useful to themselves. . . . Now, it never seems to occur to these . . . that Nature's object in making animals and plants might possibly be first of all the happiness of each one of them, not the creation of all for the happiness of one. Why should man value himself as more than a small part of the one great unit of creation? And what creature of all that the Lord has taken the pains to make is not essential to the completeness of that unit—the cosmos? The universe would be incomplete without man; but it would also be incomplete without the smallest transmicroscopic creature that dwells beyond our conceitful eyes and knowledge. . . . This star, our own good earth, made many a successful journey around the heavens ere man was made, and whole kingdoms of creatures enjoyed existence and returned to dust ere man appeared to claim them. After human beings have also played their part in Creation's plan, they too may disappear without any general burning or extraordinary commotion whatever." To tamper with "Creation's plan" was only to accelerate our journey to an end that would be, as T. S. Eliot noted two generations after Muir, more of a whimper than a bang.

It is this vision of the essential oneness of life, the relevance of *all* life to the single human form of life, that is Muir's greatest legacy to us. And to place that vision into a possibly more understandable context is the purpose for which the three Dialogues in this book were written. Some will call them inventions, fantasies. I would prefer to think of them as experiments in the bridging of time, an attempt to emphasize the lasting importance of one man's lifetime of thought and experience. Many of the words I give to Muir in these Dialogues are in fact his own, taken from his published and unpublished work and his recorded conversations. Those that are not his own are, I believe, consistent with his philosophy and personality as I have come to know them. My own responses are, of course, my own, but they are not without the visible influence of Muir's ideas. My stance—if we can call it that—in these Dialogues is that of a student to a teacher, and in so placing myself, it is my hope that what he had to give to the future will be given an enhanced clarity.

We need to learn from this man, I think—particularly now. We celebrate this year our two-hundredth anniversary as a nation. There will be bell ringing and the firing of cannons, local and national festivals, oratory full of the fire of rhetoric, and much self-congratulation. Yet even in the midst of all the fireworks we have to know that all is not well as we stumble into the last quarter of the twentieth century—that we face major decisions whose implications may not be felt for another generation, and perhaps a generation after that. That we ultimately would have to confront some change in our life-style should have been no surprise to us, although in our finest tradition we in fact reacted with a kind of wounded incredulity that the system by which we had defined our lives was not only flawed but in too many respects downright unworkable. How could the best and richest nation on earth—the nation that had given bridges and roads and dams to the world and enriched the material comfort of the human condition as never before in history—entertain the proposition that just possibly failure might await its godlike striving for perfectibility?

This is not to say there have been no Cassandras among us—the Philip Wylies and John Keatses who questioned the value of computers and conformity, the Bernard DeVotos, Wallace Stegners, David Browers, and Joseph Wood Krutches who pointed out that progress and technological expertise could destroy quite as efficiently as they could create. Yet for nearly twenty years after World War II, most of us embraced the notion that our path was true, if sometimes hard to follow. Some of us called it the American Dream. It was a powerful and compelling idea, and comforting to believe in, even then.

But slowly, inexorably, some of the hope was going out of us, even as we continued to celebrate the ordained rightness of our way of life. A quiet dissatisfaction began stirring in American hearts, an uncertainty of purpose, a suspicion of the verities we once held as self-evident. We learned to distrust our institutions and to doubt the conventional wisdom that had allowed the machinery of progress to foul the house in which all of us had to live.

We were questioning our system, to be sure, but we were even more profoundly questioning ourselves, doubting the quality and direction not only of our institutions but of our personal lives. Hundreds of thousands of our children drifted into their own definitions of what life was supposed to be, calling their choices countercultures or alternate life-styles. And millions of us—respectable, middle-class, and not young—were driven to our own kind of counterculture, finding solace (if not necessarily wisdom) in encounter groups and self-realization clinics, exploring the dark of our interior landscapes.

Whether any of this has really helped much remains to be seen. "Sooner or later in life," Robert Louis Stevenson once wrote, "we all sit down to a banquet of consequences." In spite of our last decade of violence and questioning, and our sometimes feeble efforts to resolve our uncertainties, we could not escape the consequences of all those years when we did not doubt, perhaps could not doubt. They confronted us in the form of what most of us called an "energy crisis." Others pointed out that it was more than a crisis—that it was, in fact, the result of an energy binge, a hangover of such magnitude that it forced us for the first time to come dead up against the fearful possibility that a standard of living was not necessarily defined by 285-horsepower automobiles, electric can openers, and a household temperature of seventy-eight degrees. We now had solid evidence that the dream on which we had based our existence may have been hollow all along. All the cant and clever intellectualizing faded when put against a hard, physical reality, and we found ourselves facing two questions: How are we going to live—and what *is* the quality of life? We may not resolve these questions for as many generations as it took us to face them, but resolve them we must.

What has all this to do with John Muir and the wilderness to which he gave his life? Quite a lot, I think. Wallace Stegner has called such landscapes part of our geography of hope, reminders that we are natural creatures living in a natural world, no matter how close to the angels we may believe we are, no matter what we have tried to do to that world with plastic and concrete. We prattle quite a bit about freedom in this country, our own freedom and that of mankind at large. But I am not sure that we really understand what the term means. The Hindus, it is said, define freedom as a prison in which we are equidistant from all walls. Muir understood that. More importantly, the world he knew best understood it, and it was that lesson he spent his energies promoting. Freedom is balance. Freedom is a condition in which all living things function as if they knew and respected the demanding rules of nature's wondrous game.

So we are not truly free, not free in the sense in which we have seen ourselves for two hundred years; we are only human. The world we have created in all our humanness is demonstrably out of balance, giving us too little of joy, and nothing, finally, of security. We need to change it, and if we are neither physically nor psychologically equipped to plunge naked into a purely natural environment, we must now more than ever before try to understand what wilderness can teach us of life, of balance, of quality, of freedom. It is the hope of this book, its text, its photographs, its *purpose*, that if we can someday bring ourselves to understand these things, truly understand them, then perhaps we can begin to build a world in which our dreams no longer die.

T. H. WATKINS

1861

THE LIFE, 1838~1868

The Scotch Are Hard to Kill

A coast is where the dreaming begins. It is a place where the line between old and new, fact and mystery, known and unknown is drawn more sharply than in any other landscape. It is here, where depths cannot be seen and distances only felt, that every seaborne journey, however brief, is a beginning—and a possible ending. Those who are born and reared in such a setting do not look on the world with the same eyes as inland people. When they stand facing the sea, the land is behind them like yesterday, and what they watch, eyes squinting against the brassy glare of sun on water, is tomorrow.

So, John Muir. He was born on April 21, 1838, in Dunbar, Scotland, a weathered clutch of a town whose stones were as gray as a winter sea. With green hills at its back, it faced the great North Sea, once the watery province of marauding Danes and Norsemen. Some thirty miles west of the town was Edinburgh, and beyond that the sooty warren of Glasgow; ten miles to the northwest, the wide mouth of the Firth of Forth opened to the ocean. Just outside Dunbar, crowning the brow of a tall hill, sat the towering ruins of Dunbar Castle, moss-grown and crumbling, a thousand-year-old relic that suggested all the ages down through the mists of time—of the days when early kingdoms spread and shrank, of Angles and Saxons, of pillaging Vikings and conquering Danes, of Roman armies driving the Gaels and the Picts into mountain fastnesses, of the Antonine Wall and Hadrian's Wall, of all the druidic centuries with their aimless, warring tribes. Like all Scots, the people of Dunbar carried their often bloody and sometimes terrible history like a fire in the heart, an ember kept living by the breath of fable and folk song. Above all, they remembered the generations of armies that had surged back and forth across the River Tweed in the ancient endless struggle with England, from the Battle of Bannockburn in 1314, when Robert the Bruce routed the English troops of the Plantagenet king, Edward II, to the Battle of Culloden Moor in 1746, when the army of Bonnie Prince Charlie, Scotland's last hope, was butchered by the Duke of

Cumberland and all the Highlanders either killed or put to flight.

This bitter history was part of John Muir's birthright, and to the end of his days he took a fierce pride in his heritage. There was much else that was bitter in that birthright. His father, Daniel Muir, was a fanatic Calvinist, full of a grim and righteous zeal, and he inflicted his cheerless doctrines on his family with a stubborn, pitiless tenacity. By dint of regular beatings, Muir remembered, "father made me learn so many Bible verses every day that by the time I was eleven years of age I had about three-fourths of the Old Testament and all of the New by heart and by sore flesh. I could recite the New Testament from the beginning of Matthew to the end of Revelation without a single stop." Sore flesh appears to have been endemic to life for a small boy in that time and place. The highest ambition among the boys in the town was to be a "guid fechter," and the wiry young Muir gave—and received—his fair share of bloody noses and split lips (such fighting usually followed by an additional paternal beating when he got home). No relief was found in school where, Muir said, "we were simply driven pointblank against our books like soldiers against the enemy. . . . If we failed in any part, however slight, we were whipped; for the grand, simple, all-sufficing Scotch discovery had been made that there was a close connection between the skin and the memory, and that irritating the skin excited the memory to any required degree."

It was a battered and painful way to grow up, and he never forgot it. Still, there were compensations, among them the dark mysteries of old Dunbar Castle and the brighter but no less entrancing mysteries of the sea, whose rocky tide pools held an abundance of life to be explored and whose constantly passing ships were talismans for imagined adventure. Above all, there were the Saturday afternoon escapes with his brothers into the hills and woods behind the town. (He was then the oldest boy of five children; there would ultimately be eight.) They scouted out nesting birds and field mice and foxes and sat for hours listening to the rising melody of the skylark's mating song. These headlong excursions, forbidden by his father, were usually followed by one more beating when he got home, but that did not deter him; already something free and beautiful was calling to him from the trees and meadows of his youth. "Wildness was ever sounding in our ears," he remembered, "and Nature saw to it that besides school lessons and church lessons some of her own lessons should be learned."

Something also was calling to Daniel Muir. For all his dour outlook upon life and its joys, Muir's father had been harboring a dream ever since the day he ran away from home as a teenager in Manchester, England, ever since his years in the British army, ever since he had come to Dunbar as a recruiting sergeant, married the heiress to a food-and-grain store, and upon her death married Ann Gilrye, John's mother; the dream was America, and as the year 1848 drew to a close it became an obsession.

America was much in the news in the last months of 1848 and early months of 1849, even on the windswept eastern coast of Scotland. Gold, it seemed, had been discovered in a part of America called California. Daniel Muir had no interest in grubbing around for gold, but the promise its discovery defined enlarged the hope he had carried so many years, the hope of opportunity, the hope, most of all, of land. Land *was* opportunity. Land was wealth. Land was power. Land was even a kind of nobility. And in Scotland there was no land—not even for a modestly prosperous food-and-grain merchant. America was the answer, had to be the answer, and Daniel Muir announced—announced, not discussed—his plan: he would take John and two of the other children to America with him immediately, find a suitable plot of land somewhere, begin their new home, and send for his wife and the remaining children when he was established.

In Scotland in the middle of the nineteenth century, a good wife did not argue with the dreams of her husband, and on February 19, 1849, the first contingent of the Muir immigration slipped down the River Clyde on board what young Muir called an "auld rockin' creel" of a ship, bound for America. For him, it was the first grand adventure of his life, one only slightly diminished by the parting words of his grandfather Gilrye: "Ah, poor laddies, poor laddies, you'll find something else ower the sea forbye gold and sugar, birds' nests and freedom fra lessons and schools. You'll find plenty sairly hard, hard work."

A little over six weeks later, they landed in New York. While on board ship Daniel Muir had soaked up stories of rich land in western Wisconsin, and it was here that he decided to settle, hauling family, furniture, and farm machinery west by canal barge and wagon to land only recently carved out of Indian possession by treaty and violence. Near the Fox River he chose an eighty-acre farm that bubbled with springs feeding a good-sized lake. He called it Fountain Lake Farm, and here he began to make a life in the New World—clearing the land of snags and stumps, laying in the first crop of wheat and corn, putting down the foundation of a good, solid house— while the young Muir, too young yet to work in the fields, threw himself wholesouled into the first real vacation his boyhood had ever known, spending the spring and summer in an extended orgy of investigation, scrambling, running, climbing throughout the bogs and woods and hills of the lush Wisconsin wilderness.

It was well that he enjoyed this respite while he could, for by the fall the large frame house was finished, and early in November his mother and the other children arrived. Life began now in earnest, and Muir learned what his grandfather had meant. For the next eight years his life was a very litany of work, bone-crushing, mind-numbing work, work so bitter and constant that he forever after maintained that it had stunted his growth even as it toughened his body. His father had chosen badly in his land; it was a sandy loam too thin in organic content to sustain intensive farming, and only daily effort could keep it producing just enough to maintain the family at a subsistence level. Undiscouraged, his father soon purchased another forty acres from an adjoining tract and set his sons and daughters to working it; again, in 1855, he purchased yet another farm some six miles from the original home farm, named it Hickory Hill Farm, and moved the family there in 1856.

Increasingly through the years the father himself did less and less work, devoting his energies to spreading the word of the Lord as interpreted by the Disciples of Christ, a missionary sect that had tapped into his grim religious passions. Blind to anything but the conviction that life was *supposed* to be joyless labor and the dream in which he now saw himself as a savior of benighted souls, Daniel Muir, in the words of his neighbors, "worked his children like cattle."

Muir's sisters became semi-invalids for most of the rest of their lives and his brothers were dulled and all but broken; but it was John, as the eldest son, on whom the greatest weight fell, and one can only stand astonished that he not only survived it but transcended it. His father wanted a well on the Hickory Hill Farm. Neighbors suggested that he use dynamite to blast down through the tough sandstone of the land. Dynamite was too expensive, so he sent his son John down with a hammer and chisel for day after day of painful labor chipping away at the rock. At eighty feet, John succumbed to chokedamp (a mine gas that supports neither life nor flame) and was hauled back up unconscious; the next day, recovered, he was sent back down. The winter wheat had to be harvested, and even though John was weak with fever, he was sent out into the bitter morning fields, until his cold became pneumonia, until he lay in his bed shivering and gasping for breath, fighting for days against death. "The Scotch," he remarked laconically in his recollection of these days, "are hard to kill." He lived, only to rise and return to the work, always to the work.

Somehow, incredibly, Muir continued to love the land, taking what joy he could find in it through all the years when he must at one time or another have seen it as

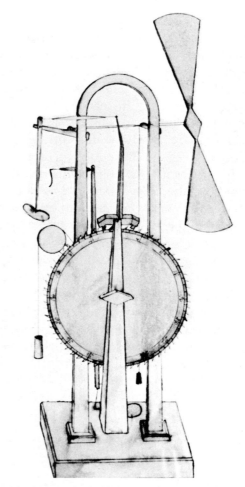

Muir's design for one of his clocks—"There's nothing else like them in the world!" a neighbor exclaimed.

an enemy, something against which all the strength of his being was pitched. His father could not destroy that. Nor could he effectively shackle the hunger and curiosity of his son's muscular intelligence. If he laid down injunctions against the reading of fiction, history, and philosophy, his son smuggled the books into the house and then took them secretly to the fields to read while the team was resting. If his father inveighed against the time wasted in the construction of wooden clocks—including one particularly ingenious alarm clock that lifted John's bed and tilted him out at dawn—his son simply rose at one o'clock in the morning, thus taking nothing from the next day's labor. If his father continued to hammer away at his narrow biblical interpretation, Muir constantly confounded him with refutations derived from a knowledge of the Bible quite as profound as his father's. If he still maintained that work was the only nobility, his son now answered that "living is more important than getting a living." Slowly at first, and then with growing speed as he went through his teens, John pulled away from his father's stifling oppression and began sensing an incipient urge to wander.

The opportunity came in the early summer of 1860. His oldest sister had married by then, and her husband had taken over the Fountain Lake Farm. Even though their father continued his back-country preaching, John's two brothers were now old enough to take on the bulk of the work on Hickory Hill Farm. When a neighbor dropped by one evening and suggested that he take his clocks to Madison and exhibit them at the state agricultural fair, John was at first hesitant, wondering whether anyone would be interested in looking at a bunch of devices made of wood. "Made of wood!" the neighbor replied. "Made of wood! What does it matter what they're made of when they're so out-and-out original? There's nothing else like them in the world." That was enough. John gathered his clocks into an awkward backpack and made his farewells—with his mother's blessing, but without that of his father, who sat glum and silent, refusing even to say goodbye. Neither of them knew it, but the leavetaking was permanent. Except for brief visits, John Muir would never again live at Hickory Hill Farm. Not for another twenty years would he spend his strength cultivating land.

Muir family farm, Montello, Wisconsin.

"*Boys are often at once cruel and merciful, thoughtlessly hard-hearted and tender-hearted . . . . Love of neighbors, human or animal, grows up amid savage traits . . . .*"

"When we first saw Fountain Lake Meadow, on a sultry evening, sprinkled with millions of lightning-bugs throbbing with light, the effect was so strange and beautiful that it seemed far too marvelous to be real. Looking from our shanty on the hill, I thought that the whole wonderful fairy show must be in my eyes. . . ."

Well John Muir dug on Montello farm.

ABOVE: Fountain Lake on Muir farm.   OVERLEAF: Cornfield near Muir farm.

Sheep grazing in San Joaquin Valley, California.

"Sheep, like people, are ungovernable when hungry . . . almost every leaf that these hoofed locusts can reach within a radius of a mile or two from camp has been devoured. Even the bushes are stripped bare, and in spite of dogs and shepherds the sheep scatter to all points of the compass and vanish in dust. . . ."

Among the Wheels of Time

Each life has in it a period of vagueness, of irresolution, of testing—a time when the question, Who am I? haunts the soul and the world is probed for definitions. These days, with our compulsion to name and classify all the warps and tangles of life, we call the search an "identity crisis." It is a hegira of mind and heart that no one escapes—and for some the journey takes all of a lifetime. For John Muir it took seven years, and if it was a psychic wandering, as it had to be, it was also physical; as he would do for the rest of his life, the young Muir translated thought into movement, and from the age of twenty-two, when he left home, to the age of twenty-nine, when he believed that the target of his life was finally seen, he moved about the world like a particle in liquid suspension, his life echoing the words of the Robert Burns he loved so passionately: "I've seen sae mony changeful years,/On earth I am a stranger grown;/I wander in the ways of men,/Alike unknowing and unknown."

Let us consider him, then, this Scottish Tristram Shandy. Physically he was not tall—perhaps five feet, ten inches—but as lean and tough as hemp, a legacy of all his years of grubbing toil. His face already sported the rat's nest of a beard that he carried with him to the end of his days, and his dark auburn hair, subjected to scissors at only sporadic intervals, whipped about in the wind innocent of pomade, comb, or brush. It was a good face that was framed by all that hair, thin but as strong and brown as if it had been carved and polished out of wood. The lips were delicate, almost female, but the nose thrust out above them like the edge of an axe. And the eyes—which were the first thing one noticed about him and, according to the evidence, the one thing no one ever forgot—they were as blue as if chipped from a glacier's heart and shone with an intensity that some took for madness and others for genius, both impressions at least partly correct since like all extraordinary men he probably was a bit of each. Filled with more than his share of the brash certitudes of youth, he ventured frequently doctrinaire opinions on any and all subjects, particularly religion, in the discussion of which he occasionally reflected something of the messianic wrath of his father. ("It appears strange to me," he later wrote to an old friend of those days, "that you should all have been so patient with me.") Against this was a sudden shyness and diffidence, an uncertainty that immediately appealed to the maternal instincts of men and women alike, as well as the charm and wit of a natural storyteller and conversationalist, the quick, sometimes voluminous spates of words delivered now with only the softest of burrs, now with all the moist, growly accents of the Dunbar boy he was.

So armed, with his splendid gadgets high on his back and a single gold coin from his mother in the pocket of his homespun pants, the young Muir hurried out into the world.

By all accounts his machines were the hit of the agricultural fair at Madison, drawing thousands of spectators and being reported in many local newspapers. (His father, reading some of the reports, promptly scribbled him a letter warning him against the sin of pride; no money was enclosed.) They also captured the attention of Mrs. Ezra S. Carr, whose husband was a professor at the University of Wisconsin, an institution whose three buildings crowned the top of a hill in full view of the fairgrounds. She was the first of the many "mothers" Muir would encounter throughout much of his life, women who encouraged, prodded, and coddled him as if they were cultivating a strange, wild flower. He became a steady guest at the Carr home when he was not out tramping about in the woods outside of town or wandering hungrily in the grounds of the university cam-

pus. He wanted desperately to attend the college but could not screw up enough courage to ask for admission—not yet.

In the meantime, the inventor of the fair's other main attraction—an iceboat named the *Lady Franklin*—invited him to accompany the boat up to Prairie du Chien and help prepare it for its first winter test. In exchange the boat's owner grandly offered to teach him mechanical and engineering drawing. Muir accepted, but after a winter in which he worked as a kind of handyman for a local hotel, in which he may or may not have acquired a romantic attachment for the niece of the hotel's owner, in which the iceboat turned out to be a mechanical disaster, and in which he received only one of the drawing lessons he had been promised, he returned to Madison, walked into the chancellor's office of the university, and in late January 1861, was admitted to the college as an "irregular gent," a classification reserved for those who had no more definite goal than learning itself.

The two-and-one-half years he spent at the University of Wisconsin comprised the total of Muir's exposure to higher learning, but it can be said that he made the most of it. In all his subjects—geology, chemistry, Latin, and Greek—he excelled, and in one instance transcended: since the university could not yet afford a chemistry lab, he proceeded to set one up in his student room in North Hall, frequently utilized by his professor in the subject. His busy hands and mind constructed yet more machines, the most astonishing of which was a singular "student's desk," a contraption that lifted a book to a circular platform, opened it, gave the student a specified number of minutes to peruse the exposed

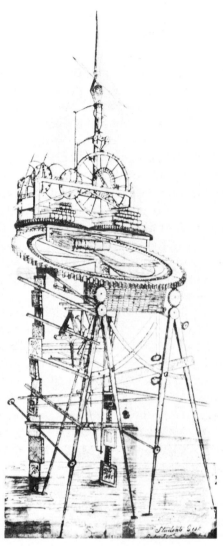

Muir's student desk, one of his wheels of time.

lesson, then moved the book around, and lifted up and opened another. This and similar devices made his room one of the university's chief tourist attractions (then and in later years). It was here, too, that he first became exposed to the botanist's craft, which he embraced with his usual manic enthusiasm, plunging into afternoons and weekends of collection and classification of nearly every wild growing thing he could lay hands on.

Still, there was little or no money. His mother sent him what she could pry loose from her miniscule household allowance, and once even his father sent him ten dollars; it was accompanied by a letter in which the old man not very subtly hinted that some of it be used to help the "unfortunate heathen" of the world—but since Muir was feeding himself on approximately fifty cents a week he quite understandably used the money to fill his own unfortunate stomach. To solve—or at least ameliorate—the money situation, he spent the winter of 1861–1862 teaching in a small country school some ten miles from Madison (during which, predictably enough, he constructed a machine that automatically lit a morning fire in the school's potbelly stove before he and his pupils arrived).

Back at the university in the spring, a little the richer, he stubbornly applied himself to another year of study, botanizing, debating, inventing, and, above all else, reading—soaking up not only what the university's small library had to offer but the material in the fine library maintained by the Carrs in their home, exposing his sponge of a mind to Louis Agassiz, Alexander von Humboldt, Ralph Waldo Emerson, Henry David Thoreau, William Wordsworth, and such ancestral conservationists as Increase A. Lapham and John Marsh. He also did his best not to think about that unmitigated horror called the Civil War in spite of the fact that the dead and dying and sick and wounded from both sides reposed in a fetid cluster in Camp Randall just outside Madison, a place to which he resolutely turned time and again to offer what help and solace he could. (For a brief while he seriously considered taking up the study of medicine, inspired by a desire to lessen the kind of agonies he had seen at Camp Randall.)

By the spring of 1863, however, he was possessed of an urgent restlessness. His college studies, as entrancing and mind-filling as they were, led him in no specific direction—nor was he ready for direction yet in spite of the fact that he was twenty-five years old. The only specific calling he felt was an undefined yearning toward wildness, which could hardly be called a profession. Nor was it something his contemporaries could readily understand; it defied the logic of the age, one in which a man was expected to enter one niche or another of a well-ordered world as a lawyer, a doctor, a farmer, a minister, a professor, a businessman—even, God save the mark, as a politician. Still it was there, that yearning, and Muir found it increasingly hard to resist. Mrs. Carr was already calling it his "good daemon," and as the months passed through spring and summer it began to possess him in earnest. He waited throughout the winter; it was entirely possible that his name would come up in what appeared would be the final draft of the Civil War, and as much as he feared and deplored the bloody futility of that conflict, he could not bring himself to run away from what he saw as his duty. But winter passed and his name did not come up, and when the wind quickened with the smell of spring in late February 1864, Muir fled.

With a knapsack containing a single change of underwear, a pencil and notebook, and very little money, he walked across Michigan, avoiding as best he could the cities of Lansing and Detroit, and crossed over into Canada, deep into the woods and bogs and meadows and lakes of the 150-mile-wide stretch of land that divided Lakes Huron and Erie. For months he scrambled in and out of the wilderness like a hairy woodsprite, a muddy specter who appeared at the back porches of the scattered farmers of the district. He offered his labor in exchange for food and talked enthusiastically of the flowers and shrubs and trees he had seen, utterly mystifying the simple folk who normally regarded any kind of plant life either as something to be grown for food or something to be cut down and grubbed out of the land so that something else might be grown. September found him near Niagara Falls, where he met with his brother Daniel (who had escaped from Hickory Hill Farm earlier that summer and worked for a while in a small broom-and-rake factory near the southern shore of Georgian Bay on Lake Huron). Winter was fast approaching and money continued a problem, so the two Muirs decided to make their way back to Georgian Bay and seek employment in the little factory.

The firm of Trout and Jay took them on—the firm and the whole Trout family, one of many that would harbor Muir in his travels. For nearly a year, remarkably, Muir remained in the small hollow near Meaford, Canada (his brother returned to the States in the spring of 1865), contentedly working in the factory and spending his spare hours wandering and collecting in an environment where, as he wrote to a friend in Prairie du Chien, "flowers are born every hour; living sunlight is poured over all, and every thing and creature is glad." Among the glad creatures was Muir himself, yet a year in one place was for him an uncommonly long time; dreams of wandering farther and farther, deeper into more distant wildness pressured him. To do it, he would need a substantial "poke," so he entered into a contract with his employers to improve the present machines of the factory and invent new ones for the production of 30,000 broom handles and 12,000 rakes, in exchange for which he would receive half the profits from their sale. "It was a delight to see those machines at work," his employer recalled, and by the end of February 1866, the 30,000 broom handles and 6,000 of the rakes were finished and stored. But on the night of March 1, the plant caught fire and burned to the ground, taking with it not only the factory's inventory but all of Muir's notes and painstakingly collected plants. His employers, uninsured, were nearly destitute; Muir accepted a promissory note (which was ultimately paid) for two hundred dollars and enough hard cash to pay for his train fare, and set out for Indianapolis still determined to put his hopes into action by earning his walking money in that bustling little metropolis.

In Indianapolis, Muir came dangerously close to achieving success in the world. Almost immediately, he found work at the firm of Osgood, Smith and Company, a factory devoted to the production of hubs, spokes, and other carriage-wheel parts. Within a matter of weeks he had risen from the status of a mere saw-operator to that of foreman and had invented, again, new machines to facilitate production. His employers were so taken with him, in fact, that in December 1866 they hired him to set up what may well have been the country's first time-and-motion study—a detailed analysis, complete with charts, of the plant's production flow. In his presentation Muir not only pointed out areas of waste and inefficiency, showed how they could be corrected, and introduced plans for the reorganization of the line of production, but advocated an eight-hour day for the workers, maintaining that his studies proved that labor efficiency declined so sharply after eight hours that the company was not even getting its money's worth (such as it was in those days) from its employees—this at a time when the *ten-hour* day was considered a major concession to the demands of labor. The company was suitably impressed, and in a plant extension put his ideas to work.

Muir enjoyed the "rush and roar and whirl of the factory," and his human side instinctively welcomed the praise and appreciation he was receiving; moreover, he was earning more money than he had ever before seen in his life. Subverted by the excitement of it all, his collecting and his woodsy excursions fell off to occasional jaunts, and the vision he had begun to nurture in Canada faded against the glitter of promotions and salary increases.

Then something occurred which Muir steadfastly maintained was nothing less than an act of God. Working on a piece of machinery with a sharp file early in March 1867, his hand slipped, the point of the file lancing into his right eye. He cupped the eye and felt the ophthalmic fluid dripping into his palm. In excruciating pain, he staggered home to his boardinghouse room and took to his bed. By evening, he could no longer see out of his right eye, and his left had blanked out in sympathy. He was blind. The first doctor who examined him said the right eye was gone permanently, and Muir indulged himself in perhaps his first and only orgy of despair and self-pity. "The sunshine and the winds are working in all the gardens of God," he awkwardly scribbled in a note out of his darkness, "but I—I am lost!" That note, and others, got to one more of the families he had collected—the Merrills of Indianapolis—and a specialist was sent around at once. The new doctor soothed his fears; while forever impaired, the right eye would heal itself well enough to see, and the left would of course come back to sight once the shock was gone.

He still had a month of darkness to endure, however, and during that time, like a thirsty man rolling a pebble around in his mouth, Muir worried at what he had almost lost, the old resolve growing with each day. "As the leaf on the ripples of the Lake, generation follows generation," he had written six years before, while still at the University of Wisconsin. "We are passing away. How great the need for energy to spend our little while to purpose." In the years that had followed, he had struggled to find that purpose, "tormented," as he later wrote, "with soul hunger." He had come close to an answer in Canada, and now, in his sickbed, harried by time and terrified at how close he had come to losing sight of all that was important to him, he came back to the determination to turn his back on orthodoxy and what passed for civilization, to go whole-souled and unafraid into the wilderness, "not as a mere sport or plaything excursion, but to find the Law that governs the relations subsisting between human beings and Nature." Never again would he allow himself to be lost among the wheels of time.

Homecoming

Early in April 1867, Muir took his first walk in the woods since the return of his sight, drinking in the beauty of the "sweet fields." He then returned to town and formally resigned his position at Osgood, Smith and Company, and went to Hickory Hill Farm for a visit. His father had not mellowed visibly through the years, still proclaiming fire and brimstone and railing against the "Deevil's work," of which he considered his son's ramblings the prime example. Upon Muir's departure, the story goes, his father interrupted his leavetaking with his mother and sisters with "My son, hae ye na forgotten something?"

"What have I forgotten, Father?"

"Hae ye na forgotten to pay for your board and lodging?"

Muir handed the old man a gold piece. "Father," he said, "you asked me to come home for a visit. I thought I was welcome. You may be very sure it will be a long time before I come again." It was a promise Muir kept. Not until Daniel Muir lay racked on his bed of death would he see his son again.

With Merrill Moores, a friend from the Merrill family, Muir journeyed down the Wisconsin River on a raft to Portage, where his brother David was busily establishing himself as a leading merchant. After managing to embarrass his brother by showing up at his store in his bare feet (he had lost his shoes to the river), Muir deposited his factory earnings with David and went back to Indianapolis with Moores to make another series of good-byes. On September 1, 1867, "joyful and free," he boarded a southbound train for the first leg of a journey he hoped would take him through the American South to the Gulf of Mexico, and from there to the great unknown of the South American continent. "I might have become a millionaire," he later said somewhat grandly, "but I chose to become a tramp!" The joy, even in recollection, was discernible.

At Jeffersonville, Indiana, he stepped from the train and the following morning crossed the Ohio River into Kentucky. He was, of course, walking now, on his back the usual pack stuffed with the usual

At home with death in the Bonaventure graveyard, October 1867.

change of underwear, notebooks and pencils, and such simple foodstuffs as bread and tea. Holding to a vaguely southeastward course, sleeping in the open when he had to and with white and Negro farmers and sharecroppers when the opportunity presented itself, bubbling with delight at every newly-discovered plant and jamming as many as he could into his pack, he picked his way across Kentucky (stopping long enough to marvel at Mammoth Cave) to the western slopes of the Cumberland Mountains in Tennessee. Disregarding warnings that bands of wartime guerrillas and outlaw blacks were still active, he climbed into the mountains with awe, for they were, he noted in his journal of the trip, "the first real mountains that my foot ever touched or eyes beheld"—a clear case of love at first sight. Standing near the summit and watching those ancient, round-shouldered ridges marching away into the mists of horizon, he called the landscape something "grandly seen, stretching over hill and valley, adjusted to every slope and curve by the hands of Nature—the most sublime and comprehen-

sive picture that ever entered my eyes."

By September 12, he was on the eastern slopes of the Cumberlands, trekking into eastern Tennessee and the southwest corner of North Carolina through a tangled wilderness of oaks, pines, laurels, and magnolias, of milkworts, goldenrods, and asters, and of briars and brambles "that come down over you like cruel living arms, and the more you struggle the more desperately you are entangled, and your wounds deepened and multiplied." Ten days later he had fought his way down out of the mountains to the gentler banks of the Chattahoochee River of Georgia, and a few days after that had crossed into the grasslands, cypress swamps, and pine barrens of the Savannah River valley.

On October 8, he arrived in Savannah and went immediately to the express office and post office, expecting to find a draft of money from his brother; it had not arrived yet, and he spent nearly his last bit of money for a cheap room for the night. The next day, the money still had not arrived, and down to his last twenty-five cents, Muir made his way out to the local graveyard, put up a crude brush hut, and proceeded to live on soda crackers and water for the next five days, his condition not enhanced by a steady, nagging fever that he had picked up somewhere along the way. On the sixth day, his money arrived. Ignoring his worsening fever, he filled his belly and booked immediate passage on a small steamship bound for Fernandina, a village on the northeast coast of Florida.

After landing at Fernandina, he half-walked, half-waded, and half-swam across the swamps and marshes of northern Florida, heading west toward the Gulf of Mexico through country that bred pestilence like swamp fog. He reached Cedar Key on the Gulf on October 23. Still refusing to admit that he was sick, he found another family—the Hodgsons—willing to put him up and laid plans to take the first boat to Cuba and, after a sojourn in its mountains, to travel on to South America. But malaria had him now and would not let go. One afternoon, after a botanizing walk, he staggered and fell unconscious. He awoke near midnight and somehow crawled back to the Hodgson home, where he was put to bed and administered doses of quinine and calomel.

For more than two months his hardened body fought against malaria, typhus, and dropsy, and it was not until early in January that he was well enough to walk unaided. In spite of the protests of the Hodgson family that he was not yet well, when a ship bound for Cuba put into the little harbor of Cedar Key, he booked passage, sailing on January 9, 1868. The ship arrived in Habana harbor on January 12, and for the next four weeks Muir lived aboard ship, leaving it only for excursions into town and for trips into the surrounding hills in order to gather plant specimens.

His efforts to find a ship bound for South America went begging. Besides, it was becoming increasingly clear that it would be a long time before he would be well enough to take on an adventure of such dimensions. Well, if not South America, why not California? The name of the state had been familiar to him since the stories of its gold had revived his father's dreams of land nearly twenty years earlier in Dunbar. Since then he had read of magnificent Yosemite Valley and of the great range called the Sierra Nevada. Perhaps a year or so in the mountains of California, whose climate was said to be capable of curing everything from the vapors to *locomotor ataxia*, would fatten him up and give him the strength for South America. So deciding, Muir took the first ship back to New York, laid out forty dollars for steerage quarters to California by steamer, and early in March sailed for Aspinwall on the east coast of Panama, crossed the Isthmus to Panama City, and boarded another steamer for San Francisco.

He remembered the Isthmus crossing, with its "riotous exuberance of great forest trees, glowing in purple, red, and yellow flowers," with great pleasure. The rest of the trip was something he refused to talk about for the rest of his life, and in his journal he only noted that "never before had I seen such a barbarous mob, especially at meals." Some idea of what it must have been like can be gained from the accounts of two earlier steamer passengers, Bayard Taylor and Hubert Howe Bancroft. "I believe the controlling portion of the California emigration is intelligent, orderly, and peaceable," Taylor wrote, "yet I never witnessed so many disgusting exhibitions of the lowest passions of humanity, as during the voyage. At sea men completely lose the little arts of dissimilation they practice in society. They show their true light, and very often, alas! a light little calculated to encourage the enthusiastic believer in the speedy perfection of our race." Bancroft was even less enthusiastic: "No man knows himself, much less his neighbor, until he has made a voyage in an overcrowded ship in hot weather. . . . To the refined and sensitive, such an infliction, from which there was no escape for days and weeks, was torture. Of all the miseries I ever experienced on shipboard, seasickness, tempest, filth, and fever included, by far the worst has been the crowd, among whom there were always some supremely disgusting persons whose presence one could not escape." Doubtless his California voyage was Muir's first exposure to the potential depravity of the human condition, and it shook him to the very foundation of his Scotch soul.

In any case he arrived in San Francisco little inclined to wallow in the delights of the city. Nourished by a steady stream of gold from the Sierra Nevada and silver from the mines of the Comstock in Nevada, the city bustled. She built up, tore down, and moved things about in a mighty frenzy, looking forward to the day when she would "annex" the United States with completion of the transcontinental railroad and smugly accepting the notion that she was the single most exciting city in the whole country. Muir was not impressed. With a like-minded companion, Joseph Chilwell, whom he had met on shipboard, he asked the first pedestrian on Market Street willing to stop and listen to him which was the fastest way out of the city. "Where do you want to go?" the man asked. "Anywhere that is wild," Muir replied, and later recalled that "he seemed to fear that I might be crazy, and that . . . the sooner I got out of town the better, so he directed me to the Oakland ferry."

Landing in Oakland, the pair walked south, past San Jose, through the flower- and orchard-filled Santa Clara Valley into Gilroy, then east across the Coast Range through Pacheco Pass, from whose summit Muir glimpsed the San Joaquin Valley in all its spring glory: "Looking down from a height of fifteen hundred feet, there, extending north and south as far as I could see lay a vast level flower garden, smooth and level like a lake of gold —the floweriest part of the world I had yet seen. From the eastern margin of the golden plain arose the white Sierra. At the base ran a belt of gently sloping purplish foothills lightly dotted with oaks, above that a broad dark zone of coniferous forests, and above this forest zone arose the lofty mountain peaks, clad in snow." The pilgrims crossed the flower garden of the valley to the foothills of the mountains, then trudged up the divide between the Merced and the Tuolumne rivers, and very close to Muir's birthday gained their first sight of Yosemite. Muir left us no notes, no journal scribblings, no memoirs of what must have passed through his mind and heart at that moment. We can only remember our own first thoughts when confronted with that splendid abyss and add a factor of perhaps ten to imagine its impact on the roving Dunbar boy.

John Muir was thirty years old. John Muir was home.

The First Dialogue

Martinez

*T*he house sits like a great brown mushroom on a small knoll at the
western end of the Alhambra Valley. It is an elegant Victorian place, topped
with the curiosity of a bell tower that commands a view of the whole valley. Below
and to the right of the house as you face east is a freeway snaking past the
little city of Martinez. The freeway is Highway 4, which is a link to the Eastshore
Freeway, which is the link to the Nimitz Freeway, the MacArthur Freeway,
the San Francisco–Oakland Bay Bridge, and all the other whips of
concrete that make up the tangle of the Bay Area's transportation network.
There is not much land left around the house now. It is surrounded by housing
developments and service stations, body shops and supermarkets. It is an
island carved out of the past; they call it the John Muir National Historic Site. It is
administered by the National Park Service and the public is welcomed.

It has been a long, wet winter, but spring is finally here. The
oak-studded hills around and behind the house are a bright, pool-table green.
Scotch broom, wild mustard, mimosa, and lilac blooms illuminate the hills and the
evening breeze carries a hint of warmth and the smell of salt—and of exhaust
fumes. You are standing on the porch of the house. It is nearly dusk, and the last
tourist has long since left. You are alone, except for the old man next to you.
He leans with his hands against the railing, his nose and straggling
white beard thrusting into the breeze, his bright blue eyes peering between
the tall Canary Island palms that flank the entrance to the house. You wonder
what he is thinking. You ask him.

After a moment he turns to you with a soft bark of a laugh. "Work."
"Work?"
"Aye—work. I was remembering that I worked here on this land
every bit as hard as ever I did back in Wisconsin as a boy, back on the old

farms. You canna see it now, but perhaps you can imagine it." He moves his arm in a wide arc. "Peach trees, cherry trees, olives, pomegranates, tamarisks, quince, figs, oranges, pecans, pears, plums, lemons, and grapes. Some were planted by Father Strentzel—a dear, guid mon—but most by myself. For ten years I worked here like a dray horse. All in a good cause, lad. Money. It meant freedom. It seemed worth it at the time. I look at it now and wonder."

"You mean now that it's all gone?"

"Aye, all but this patch of ground, this sorry remnant. A national monument, they call it." He puckers a grin at you, puts a finger against his nose, and falls into the heaviest Scotch. "I dinna ken, noo, if 'tis a' that mooch an honor. 'Tis a bit as if I hae been stuffed and propped up in a corner for the gawkin' o' the populace."

He steps down the porch. "Come, lad. Let's see how my great bonnie beast of a tree is faring."

You go with him down the path. The old man walks like an Indian, toes in, long strides. It is not easy to keep up with him. The "great bonnie beast" is a redwood tree, Sequoiadendron giganteum, obviously still in its infancy. The old man hugs it and talks to it, inquiring after its health. He steps back to admire its reach against the darkening sky. "Ye've put on weight and stature since last I saw ye," he says, utterly unselfconscious about conversing with a tree. "I planted ye, and ye outlived me. If the guid God is kind, ye'll outlive him"—he points to you—"his children, his children's children, down all the generations." He gives the tree a final affectionate pat and you go back up the hill to the house. By the time you arrive, it is almost completely dark.

When you enter the house you find it dimly lighted. It is a good house, a grand house, the kind of house that for all its size is redolent of those who lived in it and loved it—a place that adapted itself to all the joys and sorrows, sweats and shouts of life. People lived in this house, they did not reside in it. To your left as you enter is the family parlor, with a fireplace large enough for a Yule log, and to your right the formal parlor, with its patterned red velvet wallpaper. Down the wide entrance hall is the dining room on the left and the library on the right, paneled in mellow heart of redwood. Beyond these two is the kitchen.

The old man nods approval as you move through the rooms. "I have to admit," he says, "they've done a bonnie job of work here. The furniture isn't the same, of course, but close, very close. Aye, a guid job."

You climb the stairs to the second floor. On the left side of the hall is a line of bedrooms leading back to a large bath. On the other side is the large master bedroom, and in front of that, its tall windows looking east down the valley, is the study. The old man bursts into laughter as you enter this, throwing his head back in delight at the scene. A desk sits flush against the windows. It is strewn with books and papers, pencils and pens. A wastebasket to the left is piled with crumpled, written-upon sheets of paper and the floor about the desk is littered with more. "My scribble den!" the old man exclaims. "They've done it to the life, the very life!"

He steps over the rope barrier and beckons you to follow. "Mind you don't step on the papers. We must leave this as we find it." He sits in the desk chair; you choose another and face him, listening. He is still smiling. "Aye, my work habits were the despair of my daughter Helen. She typed most of my scribbles for nearly two years, you know, but when I was in the full heat of composition I would simply toss the pages behind me, guid and bad, with no thought to which was what. She finally blathered at me long enough to get me to tie the guid pages with red ribbon into a package so that she would know what to type."

One hand resting on the desk, he faces you, the smile fading like the last of twilight. "A' reet, noo," he says gently, "what is it you wanted to talk about?"

"Machines," you reply. "I want to know about man and machines."

He nods. "Aye, and ye've come to the reet mon. They once were nearly my life, you know. From a lad, I was forever whittling and planning, fitting the wheels together. There was great joy in it, and satisfaction—aye, and a kind of compulsion. Great God! there were times when I was haunted with inventions that tortured me sleeping or waking until I could give them visible form, something that could be seen or touched, something that worked. My mind and heart both were given to them."

"But you stopped. Why?"

"For a long span," he says slowly, "I believed I had given them up because of the day I put out my eye working on one. After that, I said, I would say goodbye to mechanical inventions and study the inventions of God. And that is what I sairly did, for most of the rest of my life. But there maun hae been something more, something deeper, something that cut closer to the heart of the way in which I was beginning to see the world."

You notice that he seems to be slipping in and out of dialect as he talks—not deliberately, now, as if trying to amuse or impress you, but in the manner of a bilingual person whose mind is so busy he cannot remember which language he is using. He leans forward in his chair, elbows on knees, the long-fingered hands gesturing for emphasis. "You know, not once did I take out a patent on my machines. Not my clocks, not my thermometers, not my student's desk, not even any of my factory machines. A fey and foolish thing to most people, I suppose."

"Probably. They say the wheel-making machine you invented for Osgood, Smith was used all over the country for more than fifty years. You could have made a fortune in royalties if you'd patented it. Why didn't you—no interest in money?"

He growls out a chuckle. "Weel, the fact of it was I truly didn't care much about money in those days. Or ever, for that matter. 'Twas a tool, nothing more, and it seemed to me that there was a guid deal more to life than the getting of it. Still, that was na the deep-down reason for my not patenting my machines. I had this belief, you see—and the guid God knows I believed it with all the passion of youth—that man was inevitably on the road to perfection. I believed that machines were part of that forward movement, that they would free men to pursue higher things, to learn more of God's great work in the world and their place in it. If that were the case, then machines had to be acts of God quite as much as creations of man, and therefore all improvements and inventions should be the common property of the human race. No inventor had the right to profit by an invention. It was inspired by God and belonged to all mankind."

"It's been more than a century since then. Can you still hold that belief?"

He leans back in the chair, passing a hand through rumpled hair that is half-gray, half-umber. "'Now a' is done that men can do,/ And a' is done in vain.' Burns. I dinna ken, lad, but that he was right. It's na in me to believe that man is doomed. I can't credit that God would have created such a complex and wondrous thing as man just to watch him strangle himself in his own blather. Still— it did not take me long to realize that machines were not freeing men, they were enslaving them. Inventions—aye, including my own—were appropriated by men with cold eyes and colder hearts. They robbed men of the joy of work, of the pleasures of craft and skill, and gave them nothing in return. Do ye ken what I once wrote of men from the safety of my mountains?"

He tilts his head back and closes his eyes. "'As for the rough vertical animals called men, who occur in and on these mountains like sticks of condensed filth, I am not in contact with them; I do not live with them.' Aye, I wrote that, out of a darkness of heart. I deplored the metallic, money-clinking crowds who dared defy what I felt the world should be. 'Tisn't easy to give up a dream."

"Did you give it up, then?"

He laughs, leaning forward in his chair. "No! Not really. Oh, I revised that dream of perfection, I made allowances for the reality of things, but to the end of my days I hugged the chalice of possibility—that someday, somehow, man would transcend himself."

"And now—do you still think it is possible?"

The old man stares at you for a long time, drumming his fingers on the desk. He sighs once again and turns his head to stare into the darkness. After a while you realize that he is not going to answer you. Not yet at any rate.

"There were those who believed that man never really had much choice in the matter," you say, "that man himself was merely part of a vast machine called the universe, subservient to laws and instincts he couldn't control. Do you remember what Thomas Huxley said? 'The chess-board is the world; the pieces are the phenomena of the universe; the rules of the game are what we call the laws of Nature. The player on the other side is hidden from us. We know that his play is always fair, just, and patient. But also we know, to our cost, that he never overlooks a mistake, or makes the smallest allowance for ignorance.'

The old man explodes out of his silence, thrusting forward in his chair and slapping the flat of his palm on the desk top. "Huxley—that bloodless coof! That fool! He and his kind took the work of Darwin and twisted it to fit their vision of the world. And, damme, what a cold and heartless world they would have had it be! They called it 'survival of the fittest,' but no matter what they might have called it, it was a damnable theory, a dark chilly reasoning that chance and competition accounted for all things. Oh, it was a useful theory—that I canna deny. It justified all manner of cruelty, just as my father's piety excused all manner of cruelty to his children. Should a man be inspired to destroy his best friend in the marketplace, why, he could shrug it off as the natural consequence of living in the great soulless machine of the cosmos."

"But it was a damnable theory, I tell you." His hands are now like hatchets chopping at the air. "Damnable because it ignored the one real truth of the world, the truth that lives in every rock, flower, leaf, tree, and animal—including man: it was all created by a loving God, and His love covers all the earth as the sky covers it, and fills it in every pore. God is no invisible chess player. He is all around us, in everything we touch and hear and see. All the things of which the world is made are sparks of the Divine Soul, whether clothed in flesh, leaves, water, or rock. Nor is God cold and unforgiving, never overlooking a mistake. Ye have to see, the race of men has been making nothing but mistakes ever since Adam swallowed the juice of the apple, and the race of man is with us yet. Aye—the universe may be a machine, but if so, 'tis a machine created by a God whose only rule is the rule of love. And love does not mean competition among all the forms of life, it means cooperation, the maintenance of a world in which all forms of life have their place and their function."

"And man is only one of those forms," you say.

"Aye. Unfortunately, he is the only form of life that has to be reminded of that fact. Lions and lambs dinna have to be told their place. The hawk and hare know where they are. Only man has the impudence to try to turn the world all tapsal-teerie."

"Tapsal-teerie?"

He laughs now, the anger drained in talk. "Yes, tapsal-teerie—the Scotch for topsy-turvy. Ye've just been given my famous tapsal-teerie lecture, patent pending."

In the silence that follows your answering laugh, you notice that the house itself has been speaking to you along with the old man. It vocalizes in whispers of creaking floorboards, in the muted groans of old joints and joists, and the rattling titter of ancient, wavery windowpanes touched by the wind in the darkness—an architectural conversation that accompanies and punctuates the flow of human words like some kind of Greek chorus as the night and the talk wear on. With part of your mind you listen to this murmuring undercurrent, wondering what it is the old house is saying, what tidbits from the lives of those who have called the place home would be yours if only you had the wit to understand. What secrets of the night might be told you of the life of the loquacious and lyrical old man who sits before you? Were there bawdy bedroom moments when the flesh overcame the spirit of neat asceticism he carried about him like an aura? What angers overcame him—personal angers, irritations with his wife and children, complete with shouts and recriminations? What despairs did he allow *himself in the midnight hours, what terrors belied the serenity of those agate eyes, what uncertainties welled up from the ocean of his subconscious? Were there times when he cursed his God of love, the God he saw in all the parts and portions of the earth—did he curse this God on the night that his wife died?*

The wondering is a dull litany in your brain, a running counterpart to the old man's words with their stately cadences and Godful images. Between them, they destroy time, and you are startled to see the ink of the night washed out to a deep gray by the spreading silver of the pre-dawn morning. "Aye," the old man says, "we've danced the whole night through. Come along, lad, I've one more thing to show ye."

You follow him out into the hallway and up the stairs to the attic, an immense place of gloom and artifacts. Another stairway leads to the bell tower. When you reach the top, the old man pulls the bell cord, sending a pure ringing note into the morning. He laughs silently. "That should give the park people something to wonder about. My Louie would use it to call me in from the fields for meals." The two of you stand at the eastward-facing windows of the cupola. "I loved to come up here at such times, just before the sun. Particularly in those years when I gave my life to the ranch. It reminded me, day after day, of the world I had left and the world to which I would return."

The sky lightens. There are no clouds, but the haze of the eastern horizon is thick enough to absorb a stain of lavender that slowly turns to pink and then to red against the china blue of the sky. A crescent of sun shows itself and creeps slowly upward. Below you, as the morning grows, the freeway fills with cars. The rush of their passing is like the sound of surf. "Beetles," the old man growls. "Where are they gaun in such a flichterin' rush and brattle?"

To do the work of the world, you reply. To push the buttons and shuffle the papers of civilization.

He grunts. "You asked me about machines. Weel, there you have 'em, and a sleekit, hurrying bunch they are. Better machines than my day ever knew, better than anything I could have sketched out of my dreams, better than anything I could have imagined. And they're not all. Your world is crowded with machines, some of which think faster than the men who invented them, some of which can destroy you all, together with most o' the rest o' life. But hae ye once stopped to think what they mean? Do ye ken where they are takin' ye? Do they hae a purpose? Or are they just there, clutterin' up the universe to no end but their own? Ye wondered earlier if I thought man could still transcend himself. Aye—I believe it yet. But before he does, he's gaun to be forced to answer sic questions, and answer them fast. And if he dinna, there'll be no blaming of God and the cosmos for it, lad. If man weeps out the end of his days on this earth, it will not have been the immutable laws of the universe that will have done it . It will be man himself, by choice and ignorance."

The old man's eyes burn in the morning sun.

El Capitan, Yosemite.

*"O, these vast, calm, measureless mountain days inciting
at once to work and rest! Days in whose light everything seems
equally divine, opening a thousand windows to show us God."*

Half Dome, Yosemite (viewed from Glacier Point).

Glacier polish on granite, Yosemite.

ABOVE: Exfoliating granite, Yosemite. OVERLEAF: Tuolumne Meadows, Yosemite.

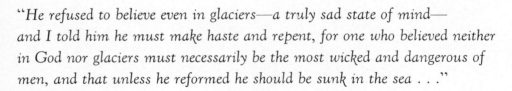

*"He refused to believe even in glaciers—a truly sad state of mind—
and I told him he must make haste and repent, for one who believed neither
in God nor glaciers must necessarily be the most wicked and dangerous of
men, and that unless he reformed he should be sunk in the sea . . ."*

LEFT: Nevada Fall, Yosemite.   ABOVE: Mist Trail, Yosemite.   OVERLEAF: Yosemite Valley after an early snowfall.

"No pain here, no dull empty hours, no fear of the past, no fear of the future . . .
Drinking this champagne water is pure pleasure, so is breathing the living air . . ."

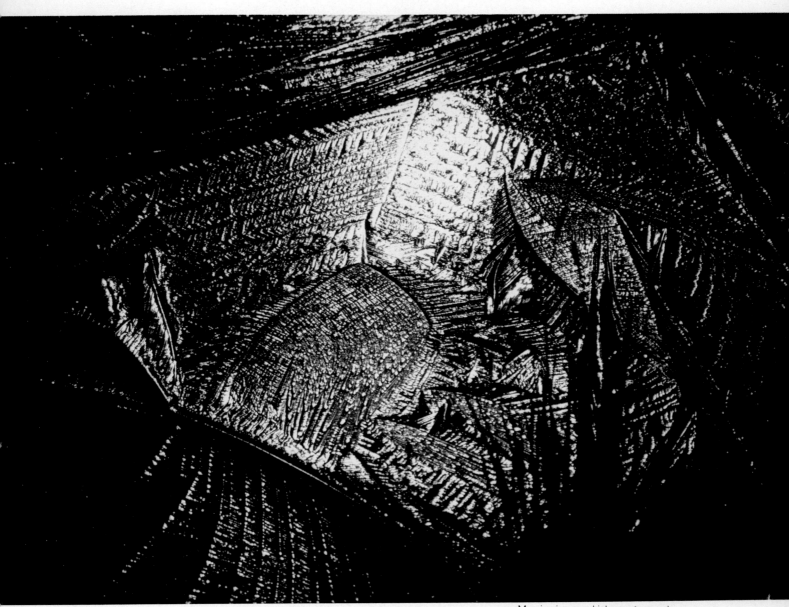

Morning ice on a high-country pond.

Fall in Yosemite Valley.

"Pollution, defilement, squalor are words that never would have been created had man lived conformably to Nature. Birds, insects, bears die as cleanly and are disposed of as beautifully as flies. The woods are full of dead and dying trees, yet needed for their beauty to complete the beauty of the living . . . . How beautiful is all Death!"

"Come next year, all of you. Come to these purest of terrestrial fountains. Come and receive baptism and absolution from civilized sins. You were but sprinkled last year. Come and be immersed!"

ABOVE: Late fall in Tuolumne Meadows, Yosemite.   OVERLEAF: Upper Yosemite Fall.

1872

THE LIFE, 1868-1881

A Particle of Dust in the Wind

In December 1868, John Muir confided intent to his journal: "Since coming to this Pacific land of flowers I have walked with Nature on the sheeted plains, along the broidered foothills of the great Sierra Nevada, and up in the higher piney, balsam-scented forests of the cool mountains. In these walks there has been no human method—no law—no rule. A strong butterfly full of sunshine settles not long at any place. It goes by crooked unanticipated paths from flower to flower. Sometimes leaving blossoms of every taste, it alights in the mud of a stream, or glances up into the shadows of high trees, or settles on loose sand or bare rock. Such a life has been mine, every day and night of last summer spent beneath the open sky; but last month brought California winter and rain, so a roof became necessary, and the question came, What shall I do? Where shall I go? I thought of the palmy islands of the Pacific, of the plains of Mexico, and of the Andes of Peru, but the attractions of California were yet stronger than all others,

and I decided to stay another year or two."

In truth, the summer and autumn had not been all aimless wandering. Coming down from the mountains after more than a month of a "grand royal trip" in the Yosemite, Muir and his friend from the California steamer took jobs in a harvest field near Hopeton in the San Joaquin Valley. When the harvest was finished, his companion left him, while Muir stayed on in the valley to break mustangs, shear some sheep, and for a brief while operate a small ferry at Merced Falls between Stockton and Mariposa. When that job was finished, he was offered a band of sheep to herd for the winter. And that was where December found him, huddled against the rain in a "dismal little hut" and spending his days chasing creatures whose principal goal in life, it often seemed, was in searching out new ways of getting killed. But he had time to watch the flowers grow as winter wore into spring, and to scheme and wonder how he could get enough money and food together to spend the entire summer in the mountains, disencumbered at last from the flock.

The means came with another band of sheep, this one to be herded up into the summer range of the mountains. At first reluctant, pointing out to the band's owner his demonstrable incompetence, Muir accepted the job when he was assured that his principal task would be to supervise the shepherding of an assistant, leaving him time for his wanderings and investigations. It was a long and productive summer for Muir, in spite of his increasing antipathy toward the "hooved locusts" who ate the land. It gave him his first extensive taste of the glories of the mountains, from the divide between the Merced and Tuolumne rivers to a long camp north of Yosemite Valley, only a little over a mile from the rim, and finally to the forests north of Tuolumne Meadows. He sketched waterfalls and collected plants, climbed trees and mountains, stood on the crown of Yosemite's North Dome, sat at the head of Yosemite Fall and watched it tumble white to the floor of the valley. By summer's end, 1869, he was ready to commit himself to this landscape for as long as it would take to learn it. "I have crossed the Range of Light," he wrote in his journal, "surely the brightest and best of all the Lord has built; and rejoicing in its glory, I gladly, gratefully, hopefully pray I may see it again."

He did. After a few weeks doing odd jobs for a San Joaquin Valley ranch to fatten his poke, he was ready to return for the winter, and nothing was going to hold him back—not even the arrival in California of his "mother," Mrs. Ezra S. Carr, whose husband had taken a profes-

sorship at the new University of California. Writing from Oakland, she had urged Muir to visit them in the city. "I could enjoy a blink of rest in your new home with a relish that only those can know who have suffered solitary banishment for so many years," he replied. "But I must return to the mountains—to Yosemite. I am told that the winter storms there will not be easily borne, but I am bewitched, enchanted, and to-morrow I must start for the great temple to listen to the winter songs and sermons preached and sung only there."

With Harry Randall, a young ranch companion he had taken under his wing, Muir arrived in the great temple in early December, where, as he noted in his journal, "after a week of resting, sketching, and general climbing we sold ourselves. . . ." The purchaser was James M. Hutchings, a transplanted Englishman who had fallen in love with the valley in the early 1850s and had publicized it diligently in his *Hutchings' California Magazine*. (This publicity had been an important factor in creating the sentiment that ultimately resulted in the federal government's grant of the valley to the state in 1864 "for public use, resort, and recreation," the nation's first wilderness park.) In 1859, Hutchings had bought one of the two rustic resort hotels on the valley floor—his stood on the banks of the Merced River, facing Yosemite Fall. Randall was hired to milk cows, drive oxen, and haul logs. Muir's duties included the operation and improvement of a small sawmill—utilizing only the many windfall logs produced during a great storm in 1867—and, when the tourist season began in the spring of

"Young snowbent sequoias": Muir drew these oddities of the Sierra in 1875.

1870, he reluctantly became a shepherd of people in Hutchings' absence, showing pilgrims about the valley.

Muir's first winter storm, which did not arrive until the middle of December, was more easily borne than he might have expected; it transformed the valley and deepened his enchantment: "Never," he wrote of his first sight of Half Dome in winter, "have I beheld so great and so gentle and so divine a piece of ornamental work as this grand gray dome in its first winter mantle woven and jeweled in a night." He approached the rest of the winter with the same barely restrained joy and carried it into the explosion of spring. Only one thing marred this first stay in Yosemite: the tourists—a gaggle of tittering, teasing Victorian ladies and dull men, whose dim perceptions of the valley did not match Muir's own enthusiasm and who thus earned his hearty contempt; "finished and finite clods," he called them, "untroubled by a spark."

When Hutchings returned in May, Muir prevailed upon him to take over the guide-work. Yet Mrs. Carr, exercising a maternal interest in exposing Muir's mind to the influence of important people, sent one after another into the valley to seek him out as a guide, and much to Hutchings' disgruntlement, Muir felt obliged to lead them around the valley. One such was a woman, and if she did not drive him to drink, she definitely drove him from the valley—which in his lexicon was quite as deep a fall from grace.

Her name was Mrs. Thérèse Yelverton, a lively, beautiful, and autocratic young lady with a tarnished past and a tenacity of will that was remarkable. Her British husband, the son and heir of the Irish Viscount Avonmore, had divorced her a few years before, charging her with adultery among other things (probably untrue), and she was now traveling about the world collecting material for travel books. Although a genteel mist has been wrapped around the circumstances of her Yosemite visit in the summer of 1870, there seems little question but that she was stricken with Muir and set out to get him however she could. Muir, unfortunately, was in no mood to reciprocate; his love was still the mountains. She would not give up on him, however, and pestered him unmercifully throughout the summer, finally begging him to accompany her on a trip to the Orient as her "secretary." Muir was not exactly well schooled in the ways of the world, but he was canny enough to know that the lady's mind was on more than literary effort. Late in the fall, when she still had not left the valley, he fled, accompanying young Randall back to the ranch on which they had both worked in the summer and fall of 1869.

Mrs. Yelverton retired to Oakland in

December to write a novel, *Zanita, A Tale of the Yosemite*, a wretched little pabulum whose hero, Kenmuir, was a thinly disguised, if not especially perceptive, likeness of Muir. If Muir ever bothered to read the book, we have no record of it. In the spring she left for the Orient without him, and a poignant goodbye letter to him suggests that her infatuation had not cooled appreciably: "Dear Kenmuir: I am just starting for China—and wish very much you were going with me. You ought to have been ready to wander away with me and see all the beautiful places. Don't forget me as I never shall you. . . ."

By then, the coast clear, Muir had returned to the valley full of resolve. "I will follow my instincts," he wrote to himself, "be myself for good or ill, and see what will be the upshot. As long as I live, I'll hear waterfalls and birds and winds sing. I'll interpret the rocks, learn the language of flood, storm, and the avalanche. I'll acquaint myself with the glaciers and wild gardens, and get as near the heart of the world as I can." More faithfully than most men follow their resolutions, Muir held to his over the next several years, burying his life in the lore of the mountains.

For the first few months of 1871, he continued to work Hutchings' sawmill, a drudgery interrupted—to his great delight—in the spring with the arrival in the valley of none other than Ralph Waldo Emerson, whom Muir revered. For hours the two men bent heads together, trading thoughts, Muir the endearing student, Emerson the inspired and inspiring teacher, open to the joys of the valley which Muir was only too glad to show him. Near the end of Emerson's stay, Muir guided the old man and his party to the Mariposa Grove of Big Trees and was gratified at the wonder Emerson felt as he stood in the midst of these giant redwoods. Muir tried to persuade him to spend the night in the grove—"You are yourself a sequoia," he told Emerson; "stop and get acquainted with your big brethren"—but Emerson's companions, fearing for his

In his Sierra journal, Muir attempted to convey the quality of a sunrise
as its light streamed through the forest of Mount Hamilton.

In another of his Sierra journal drawings, Muir depicted a Sequoia
grown in the furrow of an ancient fallen monarch.

health, talked the philosopher out of it. The party left Muir there; though they corresponded regularly until Emerson's death, Muir never saw him again.

In July, Muir gave up his job at the sawmill and set out on the first of the scores of weeks-long mountain trips he would take over the years, learning more of the mountains than any man before him—or, quite likely, any man since. With a simple cloth sack of bread, he clambered over the rocks like a mountain goat, a lithe and hairy spirit of a man who embraced storms like long-lost friends, who spoke to trees and flowers, who waded rivers and climbed cliffs and peaks with a blind, almost desperate enthusiasm, sure that the God of the rocks would protect and guide him. These were no butterfly trips, these excursions; they had purpose, for Muir was not just learning the mountains—he was chasing the very secret of the Yosemite.

A Few Harsh
and Gravelly Sentences

Sublimity defined: It probably would be no exaggeration to say that most of those confronted with the Yosemite Valley for the first time have been stricken with a single, one-word question: *How?* Certainly, it was true of the pilgrims of the nineteenth century who came to gape in wonder or simply stare in dull incomprehension, from the members of the 1851 Mariposa Battalion—generally considered to have been the first Europeans to see the valley—to the tourists who clustered on the valley's floor in the 1870s. Everything from the wrath of God to volcanic eruption was called into play to explain the valley's origins; something so spectacular must have owed its beginnings to an act of creation of equal dimensions, and the theories positively shuddered with fanciful, often conflicting speculations.

One of the most fanciful of them all was the official explanation put forward by none other than the state geologist of California, Josiah D. Whitney. In 1860, Whitney had commenced a major topographical, geological, and natural history survey of California with such able assistants as Clarence King and William H. Brewer. The first report of the survey, *The Geology of California*, was published in 1865 and contained a hint of Whitney's Yosemite theory: "The domes, and such masses as that of Mount Broderick, we conceive to have been formed by the process of upheaval, for we can discover nothing about them which looks like the result of denudation. The Half Dome seems, beyond a doubt, to have been split asunder in the middle, the lost half having gone down in what may truly be said to have been 'the wreck of matter and the crush of worlds!'"

Four years later, Whitney issued his *Yosemite Guide-Book*, an official state publication, and went even further: "We conceive that, during the process of upheaval of the Sierra, or, possibly, at some time after that had taken place, there was at the Yosemite a subsidence of a limited area, marked by lines of 'fault' or fissures crossing each other somewhat nearly at right angles. In other and more simple language, the bottom of the Valley sank down to an unknown depth, owing to its support being withdrawn from underneath during some of those convulsive movements which must have attended the upheaval of so extensive and elevated a chain." Any suggestion that the process of the valley's creation might have been less splendiferous than his colossal scenario—that it might in fact have been carved by glaciers over aeons of time—Whitney dismissed as poppycock: "There is no reason to suppose, or at least no proof, that glaciers have ever occupied the Valley or any portion of it . . . so that this theory, based on entire ignorance of the whole subject, may be dropped without wasting any more time upon it."

The man who was soon "wasting" his time on precisely such a theory was John Muir. As a student at the University of Wisconsin, he had been exposed to the glacial studies of Louis Agassiz, a Swiss geologist who had developed and pioneered the concept of a great Ice Age, when much of the northern hemisphere had been covered to a depth of thousands of feet by a vast "universal ice sheet" creeping with the deliberation of ages down from the North Pole, gouging, carving, and shaping the land into its present form. While later scientists revised and refined Agassiz's theories to include not one but several Ice Ages and not a single great sheet of ice but several sheets—and these frequently broken up into isolated glaciers—his was the first rational explanation for the shape of the land that the nineteenth century saw and for the existence of such puzzling phenomena as drift, that layer of transport-

The floor of the Hetch Hetchy Valley—"still a lake in springtime."

73

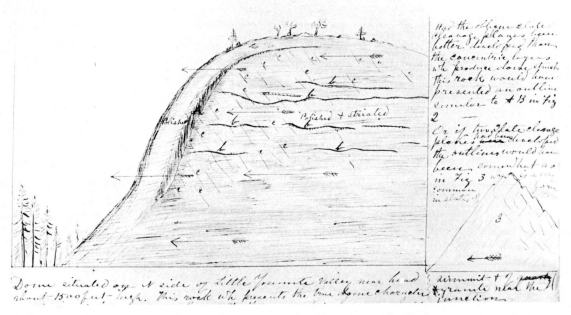

Polish and striations: here Muir examines the glacial evidence
presented by a dome of rock in the Yosemite Valley.

ed soil, sand, gravel, pebbles, rocks, and boulders that overlay large portions of Canada and the northeastern United States.

Embracing these studies with characteristically dogged enthusiasm, Muir learned techniques for measuring the flow of living glaciers, and throughout his Canadian wanderings in the 1860s kept a weather eye peeled for signs of glacial moraines and striations. By the time he reached the Yosemite, he was well schooled in glacial evidence.

He saw it in the valley almost immediately, and by the summer of 1870 was convinced that it indicated a large and complex pattern of glacial erosion, a system of ice-river tributaries responding to the pressures of weight and gravity, crawling through all the smaller valleys and canyons of the mountains to join the one great sheet that ground its way through the val-

ley itself. In her novel, *Zanita*, Thérèse Yelverton has her hero Kenmuir speak of glaciers, and we may reasonably assume that the words were those of Muir himself: "Good gracious! there never was a 'wreck of creation.' As though the Lord did not know how to navigate. No bottom He ever made fell out by accident. These learned men pretend to talk of a catastrophe happening to the Lord's works, as though it were some poor trumpery machine of their own invention. . . . Why! I can show the Professor [Whitney] where the mighty cavity has been grooved and wrought out for millions of years. A day and eternity are as one in His mighty workshop. I can take you where you can see for yourself how the glaciers have labored, and cut and carved, and elaborated, until they have wrought out this royal road."

He did indeed show people the "royal

road" of the glaciers that summer. One of them was Joseph Le Conte, a geologist from the University of California—sent to Muir by Mrs. Carr as usual. Accompanying the geologist and his party through the valley and across the mountains to Mono Lake, Muir filled Le Conte's ear with glacial observations, and before the excursion was through Le Conte had become a disciple, as he noted in his own journal: "I have talked much with him today about the probable manner in which Yosemite was formed. He fully agrees with me that the peculiar cleavage of the rock is a most important point, which must not be left out of account. He further believes that the Valley has been wholly formed by causes still in operation in the Sierra—that the Merced Glacier and the Merced River and its branches . . . have done the whole work." And, responding to the logic of what he called "Muir's discovery," Le Conte declared that "I strongly incline to the belief that a glacier once filled the Yosemite."

During 1871, additional disciples arrived, among them Dr. Clinton L. Merriam of the Smithsonian Institution and John Daniel Runkle, president of the Massachusetts Institute of Technology. Even if Whitney, ensconced in a chair at Harvard University, continued to denigrate the glacial theories of the man he called "that shepherd," a "mere sheepherder," an "ignoramus," among other charming descriptions, Muir was rapidly gaining a reputation that would soon transcend that of the stubborn old professor.

This is not to say that he then had any particular interest in a reputation; he was altogether too busy tracking down the ice-bound genesis of the valley. Risking life,

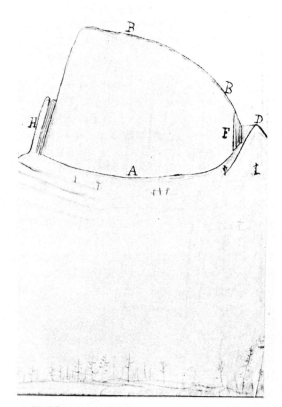

Half Dome rendered as a draftsman's schema.

limb, and sanity, Muir scoured the mountains in search of additional evidence, driven to passion by his "good daemon." Yelping with delight at every new sign of striation, at every new moraine and cirque and lakelet, at every newfound glacier, planting a line of stakes in the ice and returning to measure the rate of its movement, Muir discovered in two years of almost constant exploration no less than sixty-five small living glaciers in the Sierra.

As he loved the mountains, he was learning to love the ice which had helped to shape them. Responding to a letter from Mrs. Carr, who deplored the time he was spending on such investigations, he chided her softly: "I am astonished to hear you speak so unbelievingly of God's glorious crystal glaciers. 'They are only pests,' and you think them wrong in temperature, and they lived in 'horrible times' and you don't care to hear about them 'only that they made instruments of Yosemite music.' You speak heresy for once, and deserve a dip in Methodist Tophet, or Vesuvius at least. . . . I have been up . . . to the top of Lyell and found a living glacier, but you don't want that; and I have been in Hetch Hetchy and the cañon above, and I was going to tell you the beauty there; but it is all ice-born beauty, and too cold for you; and I was going to tell about the making of the South Dome, but ice did that too; and about the hundred lakes that I found, but the ice made them, every one; and I have some groves to speak about—groves of surpassing loveliness in *new* pathless Yosemites, but they all grew upon glacial drift—and I have nothing to send but what is frozen or freezable. You like the music instruments that glaciers made, but no songs were so grand as those of the glaciers themselves, no falls so lofty as those which poured from brows, and chasmed mountains of pure dark ice. Glaciers *made* the mountains and ground corn for all the flowers, and the forests of silver fir. . . ."

Somehow during these months when he scrambled about the mountains like a fly on a wall, he stayed in one place long enough to assemble several of his glacier letters into an article, "The Death of a Glacier," and to send it off to the *New York Tribune* in September 1871. To his delight, it was accepted, paid for, and published, and the notion that he might supplement his sporadic, almost nonexistent, income by writing began to nudge its way into his mind. In December, he described a Yosemite storm in a long letter to the Carrs, and Dr. Carr took it to the prestigious *Overland Monthly* in San Francisco, where it, too,

was accepted and paid for. In April, the magazine accepted another, and it was apparent that a career was open to him if he cared to pursue it. He was prodded in this direction by most of his friends and acquaintances, scientists and nonscientists alike. By the end of 1872 the list included not only the Carrs, Joseph Le Conte, Emerson, Runkle, and Merriam, but J. B. McChesney, superintendent of public schools in Oakland, John Tyndall, the English geologist, botanists Asa Gray and John Torrey of Harvard, and fellow-Scotsman and artist William Keith. It almost included the aging Louis Agassiz himself, who had arrived in San Francisco in August 1872, too sick to journey to Yosemite, but who nevertheless responded to a "long icy letter" from Muir by declaring that "here is the first man who has any adequate conception of glacial action." Agassiz left California without ever meeting his devoted student.

In December 1872, Muir subjected himself to a quick trip to Oakland—his first excursion out of the mountains in two years—to consult with the Carrs and others about what he should write, and by the time he fled back to the Yosemite less than a week later he had committed himself to a series of articles for the *Overland Monthly*, the set to run under the general heading of "Studies in the Sierra," and hopefully to be issued later as a book. He did not take on the assignment without misgivings, as he outlined in a letter to Mrs. Carr upon his return: "These mountain fires that glow in one's blood are free to all, but I cannot find the chemistry that may press them unimpaired into booksellers' bricks. True, with that august instrument, the English language, in the manufacture of which so many brains have been broken, I can proclaim to you that moonshine is glorious, and sunshine more glorious, that winds rage, and waters roar, and that in 'terrible times' glaciers guttered the mountains with their hard cold snouts. This is about the limit of what I feel capable of doing for the public —the moiling, squirming, fog-breathing public. But for my few friends I can do more because they already know the mountain harmonies and can catch the tones I gather for them, though written in a few harsh and gravelly sentences."

Nevertheless, he had scraped together enough "harsh and gravelly sentences" by the summer of 1873 to have completed the first two installments of the series, and he planned to spend the coming winter producing most or all of the rest. But first there would be another mountain journey, this one the longest in distance since his thousand-mile walk to the Gulf in 1867.

With Galen Clark, state custodian of Yo-

The author and artist himself trudging toward Mount Tyndall, 1873.

semite and the adjoining Mariposa Grove of Big Trees, and two other companions, Muir set out south from the valley to the South Fork of the San Joaquin River, and up its valley to the divide between the San Joaquin and Kings rivers. Muir left camp there and vanished into the mountains for four days, struggling to the headwaters of the San Joaquin, climbing Mount Humphreys, and discovering fifteen tiny glaciers. Upon his return, Galen Clark left the party to return to his duties in Yosemite, and the rest made their way across the divide to the canyon of the South Fork of the Kings River. Again Muir left his companions in camp and went on up to the headwaters of the South Fork, climaxing the excursion with an ascent of Mount Tyndall. When he got back to camp, he found his colleagues gone, leaving him neither horse nor provisions, even though they had promised to wait three days. Undismayed, he followed their tracks across Kearsarge Pass and caught up with them on the eastern slopes of the mountains, heading down into the Owens Valley. "When asked why they had left me," Muir noted gently in his journal, "they said they feared I would not return. Strange that in the mountains people from cities should so surely lose their heads."

What his companions lost, once camp was made near Independence in the valley, was Muir again. This time he was off to climb Mount Whitney. It took him six days—days interrupted by several hours lost in climbing Mount Langley by mistake and spending a miserable night amid the spires of a lower peak (now Mount Muir), feverish from an infected tooth and dancing to keep out the cold, and by a period of recovery in camp—but on Octo-

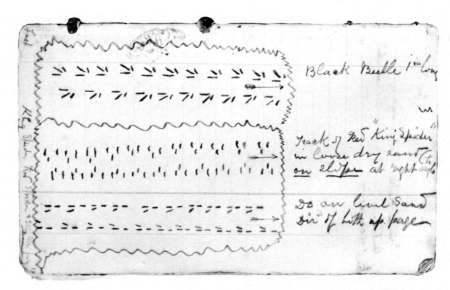

Nothing was too small for Muir's attention, including the miniature tracks of beetles and spiders.

ber 21 he reached the summit, the first recorded ascent of Mount Whitney by a direct approach from the east side. That was the last of the major projects of the expedition. After what Muir (and only Muir) called "a simple saunter along the base of the range to Tahoe," the party returned to the Yosemite.

In many respects, this six-week trip was the single most productive of Muir's mountain ramblings, not only in the distance covered (more than one thousand miles), the glaciers discovered (at least twenty), and the peaks climbed (seven or eight, though his journal is a little vague on the count), but in the scope of vision it provided. For the first time he felt confident that he was beginning to comprehend the "range of light" in all its spread and complexity—well enough, at least, to begin writing about it in earnest. "All of my season's mountain work is done," he wrote to Mrs. Carr, and as the first winter's snow began to fall in Yosemite, he

packed up his few belongings—his rather threadbare clothes, his notebooks, his handful of scientific instruments, his botanical specimens—and departed his beloved valley, his home for more than four years, for what he called "the wastes of civilization" and an extended period of writing. The "waste of civilization" in this case was Oakland, where he hoped to spend his time with the Carrs. On his arrival he found the family deep in mourning over the death of the oldest son, so he visited another friend, J. B. McChesney.

The ten months he spent in the Bay Area did not go down on record as the most enjoyable ten months of his life; he was, in fact, miserable much of the time. First, there was the very fact of civilization, particularly an urban civilization, an environment which had not known him for any length of time since his factory days in Indianapolis. The pavement, so everlastingly flat, was a pain and an affront to his mountain-wise feet. The small patches of urban greenery were no substitute for the spread of an alpine forest, and not even quick, almost desperate excursions into the hills of Oakland and Berkeley or the seashore of the San Mateo coast were enough to restore his lost wildness. The city's inevitable clatter jangled his nerves and tortured his sleep.

Second, there was the writing itself, which Muir found to be quite as mind- and bone-wearying as any writer ever has. "The dead bony words rattle in one's teeth," he complained. "Can't get a reasonably likely picture off my hands. Everything is so inseparably united. As soon as one begins to describe a flower or a tree or a storm or an Indian or a chipmunk, up jumps the whole heavens and

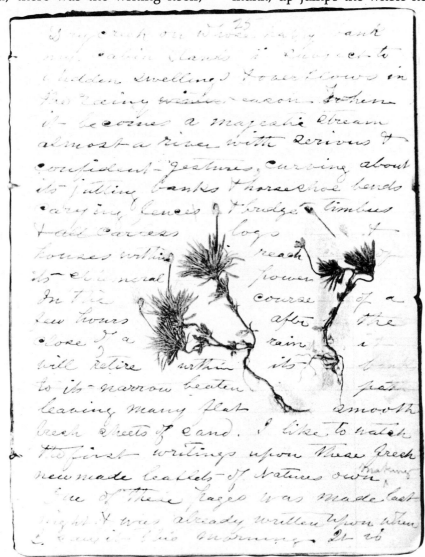

A page from Muir's Sierra journal showing the rush and intensity of his need to learn.

earth and God himself. . . ." He fought constantly against the temptations, or crutches, of the stilted phrase and the purple passage, struggling to adhere to the dictum laid down by his new friend, teacher John Swett of San Francisco: "Write as you talk," Swett told him. "Stop revising so much. You make your style so slippery a man can't stand on it."

Then there were those friends. He welcomed them, new and old alike (among the new, in addition to Swett, were poetess Ina Coolbrith, writer Charles Warren Stoddard, poet and librarian Edward Robeson Taylor, and economist Henry George, even then piecing together the theories that would emerge in *Progress and Poverty*), for a substantial part of his nature was indisputably gregarious, enormously fond of good talk and better companions. Still . . . there seemed to be so many of them, and all of them were after him to meet others, and still others. His reputation had preceded him, and everyone wanted to meet the strangely charming wild man of the mountains. His friends were only too glad to comply, attempting to change in a matter of months the social habits of a lifetime, dragging him in spite of his increasingly glum protestations to dinners and parties and picnics and even seances, the occult then being much in vogue among the Bay Area's *literati*. He endured what he had to endure, but with a deepening frustration which no one, including his much-loved Mrs. Carr, seemed to notice or appreciate.

Finally, in September 1874, "Studies in the Sierra" was finished. Muir hand-carried the last of the manuscript to the offices of the *Overland Monthly* in San Francisco, then returned to Oakland and spent the next several days aimlessly walking the streets in "a dreamy, exhausted daze," as he later put it. One afternoon he came upon a withered little goldenrod, which had struggled up into the sun from a crack in the pavement. It was obviously dying. Muir stared at it for a long time, feeling in that little death his own soul shriveled by too long a sojourn in the cities of man. He turned, and quite literally ran back to the McChesney house, said a hasty and grateful goodbye, and raced for the train that would take him back to the home of his heart, where he could be "wild once more and let my watch warn and point as it pleased."

Sierra escarpment near Bishop, California.

*"I . . . am always glad to touch the living rock again and
dip my head in the high mountain sky."*

Mount Whitney and neighboring peaks.

Cathedral Peak, Yosemite.

"*These beautiful days must enrich all my life. They do not exist as mere pictures—maps hung upon the walls of memory . . . but they saturate themselves into every part of the body and live always.*"

Mustang clover, Sequoia National Park.

ABOVE: Banner Peak, eastern Sierra Nevada. OVERLEAF: Mount Rainier, Washington.

"If my soul could get away from this so-called prison, . . .
I should hover over the beauty of our own good star. I should study
Nature's laws in all their crossings and unions. . . . But
my first journey would be into the inner substance of flowers."

Indian paintbrush, Mount Rainier National Park.

Fireweed and cow parsnip, near Glacier Bay, Alaska.

"Bears are made of the same dust as we, and breathe the same winds and drink of the same waters. A bear's days are warmed by the same sun, his dwellings are overdomed by the same blue sky, and his life turns and ebbs with heart-pulsings like ours, and was poured from the same First Fountain. And whether he at last goes to our stingy heaven or no, he has terrestrial immortality. . . . To him life unstinted, unplanned, is above the accidents of time, and his years, markless and boundless, equal Eternity."

Brown bear near Wrangell, Alaska.

Glacier Bay.

"*Glaciers move in tides. So do mountains. So do all things.*"

ABOVE: Fireweed reclaiming land in the wake of a receding glacier.

PAGE 94–95: Plateau Glacier, Glacier Bay. PAGE 96: Alaskan waters near Wrangell.

"Sunshine, Dear Louie, Sunshine All the Day..."

There can be no doubting the dimensions of relief Muir found in his escape back into the mountains in late September. "Once I was let down into a deep well into which choke-damp had settled, and nearly lost my life," he wrote in his journal. "The deeper I was immersed in the invisible poison, the less capable I became of willing measures to escape from it. And in just this condition are those who toil or dawdle or dissipate in crowded towns, in the sinks of commerce or pleasure. When I first came down to the city from my mountain home, I began to wither, and wish instinctively for the vital woods and high sky. Yet I lingered month after month, plodding at 'duty.'"

Duty done, he was free now, and glad. Yet there was a kind of sadness even in the returning, for his Yosemite work was done, and to linger in the healing moonshine and rocks of the valley was to postpone that other, more important duty he had set for himself, to "get as near the heart of the world as I can." That resolve still burned in him, but there was another

now, one brewed in the cauldron of discontent that had been his Oakland stay, one that would shape the rest of his life: "I care to live only to entice people to look at Nature's loveliness," he wrote Mrs. Carr from Yosemite. "My own special self is nothing." Muir was not one to make such declarations lightly, and in that same letter he seemed to understand that it meant an ending and a beginning: "No one of the rocks seems to call me now, nor any of the distant mountains. Surely this Merced and Tuolumne chapter of my life is done. . . . I feel that I am a stranger here. I have been gathering you a handful of leaves. Show them to dear Keith and give some to Mrs. McChesney. They are probably the last of Yosemite that I will ever give you. I will go out in a day or so. Farewell! I seem to be more really leaving you here than there. . . . Remember me to my friends. . . . Goodnight. Keep the goldenrod and yarrow. They are auld lang syne."

If it was auld lang syne for Yosemite, it was auld lang syne for much else, for that whole middle passage of his life when he moved about in the world as aloof from civilized concerns as a mountain cat tracking down its meal, from that moment in Indianapolis when he decided to set out for the Gulf of Mexico to the morning he stood on the summit of Mount Whitney, filling his eyes and mind with the stretched glory of the range. That pattern was broken now, never to be restored. The next five years would see a new one emerging, one in which civilization would set its hooks in him with increasing firmness until he was like a great, fighting salmon, running the line to its limits but never again free. Unlike the salmon, Muir accepted his semi-captivity as a necessary, if often painful, condition for the achievement of his newest goal and in time came to appear comfortable in it, but somewhere in the wildest part of his soul he must have mourned the innocence that had been lost.

Outline for a new life: November 1874 found him camped in the middle of a snowstorm near the summit of Mount Shasta, that towering remnant of the age of fire guarding the head of the Sacramento Valley, "lonely as God and white as a winter moon," as poet Joaquin Miller described her in probably the best line that wonderful old con man ever contrived. December found him wandering the rain forests and tule marshes of northern California and southern Oregon and the high country of the divide between the Yuba and Feather river basins. January found him back in Oakland, writing again, setting down the words that would entice people to look at Nature's loveliness. In April he was back again on Shasta, where he endured another storm, breakfasted on whiskey, and slid down the mountain so

The long groove left by the crash of a great tree a millennium or two before Muir.

crippled by frostbite that he had to be lifted onto his horse. He recovered in the San Francisco home of John Swett, his urban headquarters for the next several years. In June he was on his feet and on the move, guiding his friends Swett, McChesney, and Keith on a High Sierra expedition, and in September was alone on a major excursion through the southern groves of *Sequoiadendron giganteum*.

Most of the winter and spring of 1876 were spent in the Swett home writing, but summer brought him back to Yosemite for his longest stay since 1874. Again the winter and spring were lost in a fury of writing, but by the end of May 1877, he had left the Swett home for the Wasatch Range of Utah; after exploring its ragged cliffs and canyons, he wandered in and about the valley of the Great Salt Lake, climbing hills, collecting plants and flowers, and—quite as curious as any gentile—interviewing Mormon families and even going so far as to attend a sermon given by Brigham Young in the Tabernacle of Salt

Lake City. In midsummer he returned to Lake Tahoe and Yosemite for a brief stay, then journeyed down to the San Gabriel Mountains of Southern California, and back north via the coast, stopping in the Santa Cruz Mountains to explore the remaining stands of coast redwoods and in San Jose to give a high school lecture on the loveliness of nature. (It was not his first lecture, nor would it be his last; the wild man of the mountains was making his adjustments.) In September he guided botanist Asa Gray and an English colleague to Mount Shasta and Mount Lassen, then spent a week at the Chico home of California pioneer John Bidwell. In a somewhat jerry-built rowboat, he then sailed off on the currents of the Sacramento River, down through the watery tangle of the Sacramento–San Joaquin delta and down the San Joaquin to a point near Martinez.

Leaving the boat there, he walked west up the narrow Alhambra Valley to the home of Dr. John Strentzel, his wife, and his daughter, a trio he had met and liked in the Carr home some three years before. He spent a few days with the family, then returned to the Swett home in San Francisco, where he went to elaborate lengths to explain what a fine scientist he considered Dr. Strentzel to be and what a handsome, upstanding woman he had in his wife. "Did you," Mrs. Swett asked somewhat archly, "by any chance observe a young lady about the house?" Well, yes, Muir replied, doubtless boxing his ankles and looking at the floor or out the window, he had noticed someone else around the place.

He had indeed. Her name was Louie Wanda, an improbable designation which did nothing to discourage the germ of something growing in Muir's heart. For twenty years he had lived a single and, we may assume, a celibate life. After all, it was still an age in which male chastity was generally looked upon as a virtue rather than evidence of a crippled libido, a time when the fine art of sublimation was by no means restricted to Catholic priests. It takes no great twist of the imagination to suppose that Muir had found a quite satisfactory sublimation in the wilderness to which he had given his heart and body for so many years. As for rumors of his relations with Indian maidens, which are periodically revived even today, we can dismiss them as being totally out of character; he had escaped much of his Calvinist heritage, but it is not likely that he had escaped that part of it. If he could resist the refined and probably available charms of Mrs. Yelverton, it is ludicrous to suggest that he would have succumbed to the beckoning of some poor Indian girl.

The repression of his sexual urges probably had not presented much of a problem for Muir; ignoring the itch for domesticity was another matter. He was almost forty years old, an age which is quite as much of a watershed for men as the age of thirty is said to be for women. For twenty years he had lived as a kind of perpetual adopted son, borrowing from other men's lives, sharing in the love of many families, none of them his own. That he was beginning to regret the fact was revealed in one of his journal entries from his trip to the land of Mormons: "Coming down from mountains to men, I always feel a man out of place; as from sunlight to mere gas and dust, and am always glad to touch the living rock again and dip my head in high mountain sky. In Mormon baby thickets

I feel more than ever insignificant. One compassionate woman looked me in the eye with wonder. I say I've not had baby opportunities. . . . Water birds and squirrels and wild sheep are my only children. A Mormon woman tells you at once . . . 'I've nine, ten, fifteen,' and then asks: 'How many have your wives yielded? What of your fruit?' . . . I look out of the door to the mountain instinctively, and fortunately there are mountains before every Utah door, and say: 'I've not got any!'"

Neither wives nor children; only wilderness. It was no longer enough, and in Louie Strentzel he saw the enlargement of his life. In the spring of 1878 he began courtship in earnest, though slowly and more than a little stiffly, let it lull during a summer spent with a Coast and Geodetic Survey party in the mountains of the Great Basin, revived it during the autumn and winter, accelerated it during the spring, and by summer had carried it to its conclusion. One night in June, after a week of lecturing a Sunday-school convention in Yosemite, Muir showed up at the Strentzel home and made his formal proposal. Louie Strentzel accepted—and almost immediately got her first taste of what marriage to this half-child, half-man, this strange and endearing wanderer, would be like: in July her fiancé left for Alaska, not to return for seven months.

From Muir's Alaskan journals: a canoe-load of explorers navigating Cross Sound.

It is easy to understand the appeal that Alaska held for Muir. Here was a new land, a land almost totally wilderness, a land known only at its edges, and that only partly known. It had been a possession of the United States for only a little over twelve years when Muir sailed in July 1879, and was still known as "Seward's Icebox" and "Seward's Folly." To Muir, it was not folly but wonder, and from the moment that the steamer *California* left Puget Sound for Fort Wrangell via the island-studded Inland Passage, he was entranced as he had not been since his first glimpse of Yosemite. "Day after day we seemed to sail in true fairyland," he wrote in his journal, "every view of is-

lands and mountains seeming ever more and more beautiful; the one we chanced to have before us seeming the loveliest, the most surpassingly beautiful of all. I never before had scenery before me so hopelessly, over-abundantly beautiful for description." The father north he sailed, the more obvious became the land's glacial heritage, a land whose rocks glistened with such newness that it seemed the glaciers had retreated only yesterday.

At Fort Wrangell, a dismal and boggy little settlement, he made the acquaintance and quickly sealed the friendship of S. Hall Young, a missionary to the Tlingit Indians and a wilderness enthusiast whose zeal approached that of Muir him-

The discovery of Glacier Bay, as shown in a Muir drawing of November 1879.

self. The month of September was spent in exploring the coast as far as Sitka in a small river steamer, then up the Stikine River in the same boat, Muir and Hall leaving the steamer for a day's excursion into mountains still ridden with ice (Hall fell during this trip, dislocating both shoulders, and had to be helped to safety by Muir). Muir himself explored the upper reaches of the Stikine almost to the headwaters of the Mackenzie River before returning to Wrangell.

It was here that he heard of the existence of a great inland bay to the north that was surrounded by immense glaciers; the Indians called it Sitadaka, and Muir determined to see it. On October 15 a canoe expedition that included Muir, Hall, Chief Toyatte, a Tlingit Indian who would

be their guide, and several other Indians, set off from Wrangell Island for the two-hundred-mile water journey to Cross Sound between Chichagof Island and the mainland. In camp on a small inlet of the southwest peninsula that juts into Cross Sound, Muir took the opportunity to climb a fifteen-hundred-foot ridge, and from there gained his first sight—the first sight of any European—of the great ice-ringed scoop out of the land that would come to be called Glacier Bay.

For five days the party sailed among the icebergs and into the fjords of the bay, tracing the slow-plunging course of the five glaciers that fed it. Muir named one of them the Hugh Miller Glacier; another, the largest of them all, would later be called the Muir Glacier (but was not so

String-along seaborne explorers in the wet, white wilderness of Alaska.

named by Muir). Muir would have gone on to find still more glaciers and mountains and inlets, but the Indians feared the approach of winter and even Hall was reluctant, and the canoes were turned south for Wrangell; Muir comforted himself with the sure knowledge that he would be back before long.

In mid-February 1880, Muir finally returned to the Bay Area and his waiting fiancée. They were married on April 14, and the next day Muir went to work in the fields and orchards of the Strentzel ranch as manager, a job that would soon consume much of his life. But for now, Alaska still had him in its grip. He could not forget all those dreams of ice and the great naked, newborn mountains. In July he was off again for the north, sending a constant stream of letters back to his wife, who waited in the warmth of the Alhambra Valley, cuddling the knowledge of the child inside her and sharing at a distance the inescapable joy her husband found in the Great Land. "Sunshine, dear Louie," he wrote from the land where the summer sun shone around the clock, "sunshine all the day."

The Second Dialogue

Big Trees

You are standing near the Moody Group of Sequoias (Sequoiadendron giganteum, as they are now classified) in the South Grove of Calaveras Big Trees State Park, nestled in the upper foothills of the Sierra some twenty-five miles east of Angels Camp. You have followed the old man here through a half-mile of packed and shadowed wilderness along the rushing course of Big Tree Creek, a moist, cool, enchanting world of ferns and lilies and the bright punctuation of fireweed and Indian paintbrush, the whole shaded and bordered by a richness of trees, including the splendid sugar pine, whose columns rise as straight and true as arrows, whose upper branches lie over the forest like arms of benediction.

Now you are in a small clearing with the greatest of all the trees around you. It is early summer, but here in the shade near the tumbling creek the air is as smooth and cool as melting ice cream. A dragonfly, its body a thin gas-jet flame in the air, zips past you on its way to the creek. On a nearby rock a Douglas squirrel sits and contemplates the two of you, its tail straight up in full alert, its little voice chittering and clicking at you—whether in challenge or inquisition, you cannot tell. Somewhere in the distance a woodpecker hammers at a hollow log, the sound like the rapid blows of an axe. The trail to this place has not been smoothed and formally marked like the others, and except for these creatures you and the old man are alone in the clearing. He stands against the nearest of the six trees of the Moody Group, his uptilted beard touching the bark, his palms pressed flat against it, as if he were listening and feeling for the immense tree's pulse. He says nothing for a very long time, then turns halfway toward you, leaving one hand on the tree. He seems to be expecting you to speak, knows that you want to.

You tell him of a story related to you by a friend who learned that you were coming to see the Big Trees. When he was a young child, little more than a toddler, he found himself lost one night in a crowd of strangers. From his knee-level vantage point, they were not people at all; they were simply legs—a dense forest of legs, huge legs that shifted and bent and moved, blocking his way and confounding his sense of direction. His mother soon found him, of course, and his fear melted in the familiar warmth of her arms.

"But the first time he saw these trees," you say to the old man, "he was suddenly overwhelmed again with all that terror he had felt as a child. He's never been back."

The old man snorts, but not in amusement. "And you, lad? Is that how ye regard these trees?"

"Not really. Yet I can understand what he saw here—the legs of giants, the faces lost in the sky."

His response does not come immediately. He removes his hat and runs a hand through his hair as he wanders from the tree to the rock where the squirrel sits. For a moment the squirrel seems to consider defending its position with physical violence but at the last second opts for discretion and leaps from the rock, skittering across the duff to a nearby dogwood where it clings to a swaying branch, scolding and cursing. The old man watches it as he sits, chuckling softly. "Weel, my little impudent beastie—do ye think every stone and tree is your ain, now? Hae ye no room in your warl' for the likes of us?" He puts his hat back on and pats the space on the rock next to him. "Sit down, lad, sit down. You know, this rock probably is his property. I'll wager we're sitting on top of a cache." He drops to his knees and fishes around among the duff and dirt beneath the rock and soon digs out a long, narrow cone. "Aye, just as I thought. He was protecting his ain—and he has reason enough to distrust the race of men."

"Why is that?"

"In the 1850s and 1860s the sequoia was unco popular, a faddish sort of thing. Everyone wanted one. As a result, men came up into the groves and robbed the squirrels' winter hordes of their cones, selling them for seed. A good many of the trees were planted around the world, especially in England, where they called them Wellingtonia, after the hero of Waterloo. I'm sure that experience was handed down from generation to generation, and in the squirrel-memories of these little creatures men are just thieves."

"'O wad some Pow'r the giftie gie us,'" you offer, "'To see oursels as others see us!'"

"Augh! mon, yeer accent's terrible!" the old man groans. "Do ye know the rest of that quatrain?"

"No."

"'It wad frae mony a blunder free us,/And foolish notion.' Man is a verra bundle of foolish notions, particularly when he approaches nature. I was thinking on that when ye were telling me of your friend's dream."

"Dream or memory, it didn't seem foolish to him—just terrifying."

He lifts a placating hand. "Aye, I'm sure it was, and I don't discount that. Nor was that the foolishness I was talking about. Man carries such a hopeless lot of baggage with him when he enters the wilderness. Whole generations of fear and mistrust are packed into his mind, rolled-up symbols and folded metaphors. With all that clutter, he canna see the world of nature for what it is. What he sees is colored by all that, wrapped in it like smoke. And seeing that way, he robs himself of much glory. It's an old problem. In my own time, I found it all around me. I look back on it now and sometimes think I spent half my life trying to correct all the Ruskin brattle that was loose in the world."

"Ruskin?"

"John Ruskin. One of the best writers the English language ever saw, and one of the best philosophers of his age, except when he put his mind to nature, as he did too often for my tastes. His influence was just pernicious, tainting the way in which people looked and felt about wilderness." The old man is standing now, pacing up and down and gesticulating in front of you. You want to look over your shoulder, half expecting to see a circling crowd gathered to listen to him.

"Consider this, lad. For more than two thousand years men had taken the Book of Genesis literally. 'And God blessed them, and God said unto them, Be fruitful, and multiply, and replenish the earth, and subdue it; and have dominion over the fish of the sea, and over the fowl of the air, and over every living thing that moveth upon the earth,' the Bible said, and men plunged ahead, subduing the earth and exercising dominion. No one tried to understand the earth, except where understanding might be used for something. Ruskin knew this and knew what had been done to the earth as a consequence. 'There was a rocky valley between Buxton and Bakewell,' he once wrote, 'divine as the vale of Tempe. . . . You enterprised a railroad . . . you blasted its rocks away. . . . And now, every fool in Buxton can be at Bakewell in half-an-hour, and every fool in Bakewell at Buxton.'

"Aye, he knew what harm the lack of understanding had caused—and yet he perpetuated it in his writings. He traveled in the world of nature tethered by ropes and chains manufactured in the mills and forges of convention. He was like a mouse beneath a huge bell-glass made of the heaviest and most opaque stuff in the universe, and through it his contemplation of wildness was distorted. Nature, according to Ruskin, was the joint work of God and the devil, made up of alternate strips of good and evil. Beside every mountain angel he set a mountain devil, so that the blackness of the one might be emphasized by the whiteness of the other. He had a perverse interest in what he saw as the blackness of nature, and his work swam in dark images, of 'mountain gloom,' and 'the blasted trunk, and the barren rock, the moaning of the bleak winds, the solemn solitudes of moors and seas, the roar of the black, perilous, merciless whirlpools of the mountain streams.' Great God, what a landscape of doom he gave the world! Neither love nor understanding in it at all."

The old man pauses, looking up to the height of the trees. "Ruskin never seemed to understand that he was violating his own principles. Have ye ever heard of the Pathetic Fallacy?"

"Yes, but I'm not sure I know what it means."

"Well, it was Ruskin's own. 'All violent feelings produce in us a falseness in all our impressions of external things.' That's what he wrote, and he called his theory the Pathetic Fallacy. It was a fallacy, right enough, but man is more arrogant than pathetic in holding it, I think. It is most sairly a part of those attitudes that would destroy wildness. If a lumberman looked upon trees as something put upon the earth so that he might cut them down to his profit, or if a mining man looked upon the rocks of the mountains as something put there so that he could blast the treasure out, or if a sheepman looked upon the grass of the meadows as something whose only logical purpose was to fill the bellies of his greedy beasts, then Ruskin and his ilk, for all theer cantin' words, looked upon all God's beauty as being intellectually useful. A convenience, don't you know, something put there to provide grist for theer rhetorical mills. Now, can ye look at these trees here and truly believe that theer purpose in life is to provide symbols and metaphors for man—any more than they were put here to give him lumber?"

"No, I don't suppose I can."

"Aye, of course ye can't. They hae a purpose, reet enough, but it has nothing to do with man and his petty, careless uses. Look at this, now." He holds the long cone dug out of the squirrel's cache. Pulling out a small penknife, he carves away at it for a few moments, shakes something out of it into his palm, puts the knife away, and reaching down between his knees, tucks the cone back under the rock. He holds his palm out to you. In it is resting a tiny pile of pellets. They are roughly oval in shape and perhaps an eighth of an inch in length; a crease divides each of them, giving it the appearance of very small lips. "Can ye fathom what these are?" the old man asks.

You make the obvious guess. "Sequoia seeds." You are astonished at their size. They are hardly larger than bits of dust.

The old man nods. "For maybe as long as twenty years these seeds have been in their cone, until it finally fell or yon squirrel snipped it off the parent tree. For twenty years they have been waiting, waiting to touch the earth." He stood and scattered the seeds in a broad semicircle. "With luck and proper conditions, perhaps one out of ten of these will take root, and only a few will survive beyond that. Follow me, lad." He leads you back on the path you have come until you arrive at the Louis Agassiz tree, a little less than a quarter of a mile from the Moody Group. The old man's eyes are on the ground all around the base of the great tree, said to be the largest in sheer bulk of all the trees in the grove. When he finds what he is looking for, he runs toward it and drops to his knees. "Come here, lad. Look at this."

You join him. He is peering at a small green shoot that thrusts perhaps two inches above the thick duff of the forest floor. At its top it has branched into four tiny sprouts, and it looks for all the world like a miniature palm tree. "I thought I saw this on the way in," the old man says. "Remember, now, for maybe twenty years the seed that produced this bonnie brave flicker of life hung from its tree,

107

waiting. That's what—half of the life you've lived already?"

"Yes, just about,"

"For you, twenty years is a long time. For this little shoot, that wasn't even a beginning to life. Its life began only this last spring. It survived the rains. If it survives the heat of the summer, if its tiny root reaches far enough down for moisture and the mineral richness of the soil, if it stands up to the winter rains and snows, if it isn't scorched by fire, it will hae grown to maybe four or five inches by next spring. In five years, five healthy years, it may be three or four feet high. By the time you die—in, say, another forty years—it may be fifty or sixty feet high."

You look up at the reach of the Louis Agassiz tree. "How long before . . . ?"

The old man has watched your gaze. "Three thousand years, at least. I once counted four thousand annual growth rings in an old fallen giant. Four thousand years."

"How long before they stop growing? How long before they die?"

"No one knows, lad. Oh, fire will sometimes kill them, or the winds blow them down. But a natural death, like men—no one knows when that happens. Man hasn't been around these trees long enough to find out. He only knows that the oldest of them are still growing, still adding their layers of girdling life around their trunks, still sending their seeds into the wind, still sending their great hairy roots into the acres of earth around them. Another four thousand years, another ten thousand, until man and all his works are gone, until the ice comes again—no one knows."

He takes your hand. "Here, touch it, feel this stubborn sliver of life."

The shoot is smooth and cool, inexpressibly delicate.

The old man grips you by the shoulder with intensity and surprising strength. "Do ye ken what I've been telling ye, lad? About the arrogance of man when he makes all nature serve his tiny purposes? This seedling has a purpose, and all its leaves to come, it roots, its cells, all its being is dedicated to that purpose—to life, to growth, to the manufacture of time. Ye're not touching a potential source of lumber or some puny symbol meant to explain away dreams. Ye're holding forever in your hands."

ca. 1910

THE LIFE, 1881~1914

In a Cave of Shadows

Throughout his second Alaska trip in the summer and fall of 1880, Muir was nagged by what we may assume was a portion of guilt in having left his new—and newly-pregnant—wife in the hills of California while he went off to chase glaciers. The guilt is suggested by the sheer volume of letters he sent back to her almost daily, far more than he had written when they had merely been engaged, chatty, informative letters which constantly reassured her of his continuing health, inquired after hers, and repeatedly declared his love and his loneliness. It was suggested, too, by a presentiment he had picked up along the way, the feeling, which hovered in the back of his mind throughout most of his trip, that all was not well with her. (In this he was right; only a week after his departure, Louie had taken a stairstep fall and for several days had lain in bed in fever and pain, absolutely refusing to allow her father to send for Muir.) He was pursuing his work, the work he had assigned himself so many years before, but a very human uncertainty must have haunted his

mind—the possibility that he was using it as an excuse to avoid the responsibilities he had assumed upon marriage. He was, after all, Calvinist-born and Calvinist-bred, and the sense of duty ran in his veins with a purely Scottish fierceness.

But the love of wildness that coursed through him quite as fiercely could not be resisted, not yet, and if we detect a certain vague uneasiness in his letters home, there was much joy and enthusiasm in them also. "I am back in my old quarters," he wrote from Fort Wrangell in the middle of August, "and how familiar it all seems! —the lovely water, the islands, the Indians . . . the jet ravens prying and flying here and there, and the bland, dreamy, hushed air drooping and brooding kindly over all. . . . Instead of coming here direct from Sitka we called at Klawak on Prince of Wales Island for freight . . . which detained us a day. We arrived here last evening at half-past ten. Klawak is a fishing and trading station located in a most charmingly beautiful bay, and while lying there, the evening before last, we wit-

"Oonalaska" (Unalaska) in the Aleutian chain, the last stop before entering the forbidding Bering Sea.

nessed a glorious auroral display which lasted more than three hours. . . . It was all so rare and so beautiful and exciting to us that we gazed and shouted like children at a show, and in the middle of it all, after I was left alone on deck at about half-past eleven, the whole sky was suddenly illuminated by the largest meteor I ever saw. I remained on deck until after midnight, watching."

At Wrangell, Muir made contact again with his companion of the previous year, S. Hall Young, and the two of them put together another canoe expedition for the north, this one marked by the absence of Chief Toyatte, who had been killed in a tribal squabble, and the presence of one Stickeen, a scruffy, black Indian dog, which had adopted Young. Muir missed old Toyatte and grumbled about the dog, which he dismissed as "an infernal nuisance," just a "helpless wisp of hair, a soft

little lap-midget." But Young insisted on bringing the dog along, and the unlikely exploring expedition set out with Stickeen curled asleep on his master's coat.

For two weeks they slowly explored northward, entering Sum Dum Bay (now Holkham Bay) to examine the fjords and glaciers of its deepest thrust into the land, and traveling up Stephens Passage to the present site of Juneau, where they stayed long enough for Muir to point out to a couple of half-breed prospectors, Joe Juneau and Joe Harris, where gold might be found in a nearby creek bed (it was, and in a few years Juneau became Alaska's first boom town). By August 29, they had made their way west through Cross Sound, past Glacier Bay, and that night made camp just inside Taylor Bay on the north shore of the sound, the last anchorage before the open Pacific. At the upper end of the bay was Taylor Glacier, and it

An "Esquimo" belle, mother, and hunter,
as drawn by Muir in his journal.

two of them hiked toward the mountain of ice. Under a gray mantle of clouds and in frequent rain squalls, they climbed to the surface of the glacier and began tracing its boundaries, crossing through miles of sharp, "flame-shaped waves of ice" and over a tangled maze of crevasses. When he noticed that Stickeen's paws were cut and bleeding, Muir wrapped them in handkerchiefs, marveling at the dog's pluck.

By mid-afternoon, Muir decided they had gone as far as they could for one day, and turned back toward camp. But while they were still some fifteen miles from safety, they found themselves confronting a great split in the ice, a crevasse forty or fifty feet wide and hundreds of feet deep. It was late. Above them, a "roaring storm had all the sky to itself," and it appeared they would have to spend a stormy night on the exposed ice, an ordeal not even the incredibly durable Muir might have been able to survive. "No sunbeam ever sounded its depths," he wrote of the crevasse in his journal. "Death seemed to lie brooding forever in the gloom of the chasm—a grave ready made, neither land nor sea, blue as the sky and as pure, capacious enough for the largest army that ever fought and bled. . . ."

Fortunately, he spotted a sliver of an ice bridge in the depths of the crevasse. Cutting steps in the wall of the chasm with his hatchet, Muir inched down to the bridge, shinnied cautiously across it, then cut his way back up the other side. Once safely up, he called encouragement to Stickeen, who stood trembling in fear on the opposite side of the crevasse. Slowly, painfully, the dog edged down the steps, tightroped across the bridge, pulled himself up to the waiting Muir, then bounded past

was here that Muir experienced one of the most profoundly moving episodes in his entire life.

For days, the dog Stickeen had haunted Muir's tracks, following him everywhere in spite of scoldings and pretended blows. The morning of August 30, when Muir decided to explore the Taylor Glacier, was no exception, and after a "breakfast of bread and rain" and an unsuccessful attempt to shoo the dog back to camp, the

Jaroochah, an Alaskan native of Muir's acquaintance.

him in a panic of deliverance. "Such a gush of canine hallelujahs burst forth on the safe side of the gulf of ice!" Muir wrote. "How eloquent he became, though so generally taciturn—a perfect poet of misery, and triumphant joy! He rushed round and round in crazy whirls of joy, rolled over and over, bounded against my face, shrieked and yelled as if trying to say, 'Saved, saved, saved!'" At ten o'clock that night, half-frozen and exhausted, the two staggered into camp. For the rest of the trip, on water, land, and ice, they were inseparable, and there was no more scolding from Muir.

At Sitka in the middle of September, Muir and Stickeen were parted, Muir heading home on the monthly steamer to Portland. Muir never saw the dog again; nor did he forget him and those terrible, testing hours on the ice of Taylor Glacier. He had been given, he believed, a "deep look 'ben the heart'" of a fellow creature, and it brought him that much closer to the firm conviction that all life on the earth was as one. "Stickeen's homely clay was instinct with celestial fire," he wrote, "had in it a little of everything that is in man; he was a horizontal man-child, his heart beating in accord with the universal heart of Nature. He had his share of hopes, fears, joys, griefs, imagination, memory, soul as well as body—and surely a share of that immortality which cheers the best saint that ever walked on end. . . ." And in 1909, Muir gave his little black companion of the ice a share of immortality in *Stickeen*, still one of the most widely read dog stories ever published.

Back in the Alhambra Valley, Muir threw himself into the drudgery of orchard ranching with the same energy he would have given a climb up Mount Whitney—if not quite as much joy. His father-in-law had given Muir and his wife a sizable piece of the Strentzel land as a wedding gift; Muir leased yet another parcel and set to working them both, harvesting the autumn fruit, pruning the winter trees, planting the spring ground. On March 25, 1881, their first child was born, a girl. They named her Annie Wanda, and driven now by an increased sense of duty, Muir worked himself like a serf. By April he weighed only a little more than 100 pounds and had developed a steady, hacking dry cough. In March he had received an invitation from the officers of the revenue cutter *Thomas Corwin* to accompany them on a journey into the Arctic Circle in search of the *Jeannette* and her thirty-three-man crew which had set out to find the North Pole in 1879 and had not been heard from in almost two years. Muir had turned down the offer, but when his wife heard about it, she insisted that he go; for months she had watched her husband wreck himself on the land and knew that only the healing taste of wildness would bring him back to weight and health.

On May 4 the *Thomas Corwin* steamed out of the Golden Gate, and Muir was on board. It would be the last major expedition he would take in more than seven years—and one of the longest in distance and time in all his life. He did not return until October, and by that time, with his shipmates, he had seen more of the polar wilderness than any men of the age. After passing through the Aleutian Chain at Unalaska, the ship plowed through the storm-ridden Bering Sea to Saint Matthew Island, on to Saint Lawrence Island, and from there to Saint Michael, a tiny outpost on the southern shore of Norton Sound in far western

Landing at Wrangel Land, 1881: Muir and his companions were the first Europeans to walk this strange island.

Polar bear profiles from the Alaskan journal, 1881.

Alaska. Storing fuel and supplies, they steamed from Saint Michael through the Bering Strait and into the ice-clogged Arctic Ocean, arriving in June.

For the next two and one-half months, the *Thomas Corwin* patrolled the great white sea of the north in search of the *Jeannette*, touching at the East Cape of the Siberian Peninsula (where Muir, predictably enough, promptly climbed a three-thousand-foot mountain), at Herald Island, four hundred miles north of the Siberian coast (which island Muir traversed), and finally, fifty miles farther north, at the large island of Wrangel Land (on which Muir and the rest were the first white men to set foot).

In October the ship arrived at Point Barrow, a knuckle of land on the northernmost coast of the Alaskan mainland, where it was decided to abandon the search as hopeless. Winter was beginning to swell the huge north pack of Arctic ice, and the rescue mission itself might be in trouble if it stayed too long. The ship turned south for Unalaska, and from there to San Francisco. Months later it was learned that the *Jeannette*, having been trapped in the ice off Herald Island for nearly two years, had sunk, and her crew had attempted to make it across and through the ice to the inland settlements of the Siberian coast; a handful survived.

Upon Muir's return, the Alhambra ranch had him, and would keep him for the next several years. Except for quick summer trips to Yosemite, he would do no wilderness traveling; except for letters, he would do no writing. He was committed, in body and mind if not in soul, to the development of the ranch and the making of money, and over the protestations of his wife he kept at it stubbornly, re-creating in middle age the bitter toil of his youth. It was a self-imposed exile, but it was an exile, and not even the compensations of domestic life (another girl was added to the family in 1886) could fully make up for

115

the life he had put behind him. "Time partially reconciles us to anything," he later wrote. "I gradually became content—doggedly contented, as wild animals in cages." His wife complained that he grew "shadowy" day by day, and in truth his life had become something lived in a cave of shadows, of work, of repressed frustration, of illness (his cough was back, and his new daughter, Helen, was from birth frail and sickly), and even of death. Within a few months of one another, Muir's nephew, a brother-in-law, and a sister-in-law all died, and one evening in August of 1885, he looked up from a book he was reading and announced to his wife that he had to go east, that if he didn't go now he would never see his father alive again. He left at once.

After giving himself the gift of a week in Yellowstone ("Only one week in the Rocky Mountain wilderness for John Muir!" his wife wrote him. "Oh, my beloved, you are cruel to yourself."), he continued to Portage, Wisconsin, where his mother, a brother, and two of his sisters now lived. He convinced them that Daniel Muir, now living with one of his daughters in Kansas City, was dying, though he had no proof beyond his presentiment. Leaving his brother and one of the sisters with railroad fare and instructions to join him in Kansas City (his mother was too frail to travel, and the other sister too sick), Muir then went to Lincoln, Nebraska, where he persuaded his other brother to come with him and left word for the remaining two sisters, both of whom lived in Nebraska, to come immediately.

What these seven of Daniel Muir's eight children found when they had gathered in Kansas City was a dying old man, as Muir had predicted. "Father is very feeble and helpless," Muir wrote to his wife. "He does not know me, and I am very sorry. He looks at me and takes my hand and says, 'Is this my dear John?' and then sinks away on the pillow exhausted, without being able to understand the answer. This morning when I went to see him and was talking broad Scotch to him, hoping to stir some of the old memories of Scotland . . . he said, 'I don't know much about it noo,' and then added, 'You're a Scotchman, aren't you?' When I would repeat that I was his son John that went to California long ago and came back to see him, he would start and raise his head a little and gaze fixedly at me and say, 'Oh, yes, my dear wanderer,' and then lose all memory again. . . ."

Late in the evening of October 6, Daniel Muir, tradesman, farmer, evangelist, and the hardest taskmaster, excepting himself, that John Muir had ever known, drifted away into his final sleep. "Few lives that I know were more restless and eventful than his," Muir wrote of his father, "few more toilsome and full of enthusiastic endeavor onward towards light and truth and eternal love through the midst of the devils of terrestrial strife and darkness and faithless misunderstanding that well-nigh overpowered him at times and made bitter burdens for us all to bear. But his last years as he lay broken in body and silent were full of calm divine light, and he oftentimes spoke . . . of the cruel mistakes he had made in his relations toward his children, and spoke particularly of me, wondering how I had borne my burdens so well and patiently. . . ." Daniel Muir was dead, and buried with him was the sour kernel of resentment his son John had carried for nearly thirty years.

The ranch work went on, undiminished and seemingly endless. In the spring of 1887, he accepted his first writing job in years, the editing of and contributing to a collection of natural history essays called *Picturesque California*. The only way he could work on it at all was to lock himself in a hotel room in San Francisco, away from the pressures of the ranch. But even then, the work went badly; the fire seemed to have gone out of his prose. His daughter Helen went through one of her many ill periods, and by the end of the summer Muir was visibly discouraged. "I am all nerve-shaken and lean as a crow— loaded with care, work, and worry," he wrote to his brother David. "The care and worry will soon wear away, I hope, but the work seems rather to increase. There certainly is more than enough of it to keep me out of mischief forever." Out of mischief, perhaps, but more importantly, out of wilderness.

The degree of his starvation may have been emphasized when S. Hall Young, his companion of two Alaskan trips, unexpectedly arrived at the ranch in the spring of 1888, positively reeking of mountains and glaciers. "Ah! my friend," Young remembered hearing him cry, "you have come to take me on a canoe trip, have you not? My weariness of this humdrum, work-a-day life has grown so heavy it is like to crush me. . . . And for money! Man! I'm like to die of the shame of it." There was no canoe trip, only a long night of good talk, but Muir's longing was stimulated to an almost unbearable level.

He satisfied some of that longing with a two-week trip to Mount Shasta in June,

and a good deal more of it in July and August, when he journeyed to Mount Rainier with artist William Keith, joining a team of men determined to make the sixth recorded ascent of the mountain. Keith, no enthusiast about mountain climbing, stayed behind to sketch, but Muir went with the rest. ("Did not mean to climb it," he wrote his wife, "but got excited, and soon was on top.") After standing on the top of the first mountain peak his feet had known in several years, he gamboled back down to camp, "heart and limb exultant and free." When he returned to the Alhambra Valley, he found his wife determined to free both his heart and limbs from the demands of the ranch. "A ranch that needs and takes the sacrifice of a noble life, or work," she had written militantly while he was on his trip, "ought to be flung away beyond all reach and power for harm," and she immediately began advocating the idea of either selling their portion of the ranch or leasing it out to some other farmer.

Louie Muir's campaign took more than two years, but it succeeded. Muir put in another full year of work on the ranch (and on finishing his contributions to *Picturesque California*), but spent all of the summer of 1890 on another trip to Alaska, most of which was devoted to the exploration of the glacier that now bore his name in Glacier Bay. At the end of October 1890, John Strentzel died, and the Muir family moved into the large, cupola-topped house Strentzel had built in 1882. By the spring of 1891, after ten years of almost constant work, Muir had accumulated $250,000—"more money," he recalled, "than I thought I would ever need for my family or for all expenses of travel and study, however far or however long continued." He sold part of his land, and the problem of who might be found to lease, on a profit-sharing basis, the rest of the property as well as manage Mrs. Strentzel's portion was solved when one of Muir's brothers-in-law, John Reid, grew tired of trying to make a Nebraska homestead pay and decided to move to California. By summer all arrangements had been made, and Muir was at last free to pursue his real work.

The time was right, for there was real work to be done.

Any Fool Can Destroy Trees

Free of the responsibilities of ranch management in 1891, Muir's life was now ready to take another firm shift, and this one would govern its course to the end of his days. He was now a public man, fighting in a public cause, and his remaining years would be the busiest and most productive in his whole life. Almost everything—his family life (within reason),even his pursuit of wildness—would be subordinated to the cause of *saving* wilderness, not just understanding it, for Muir, like many others in America, had come to learn by now how very little there was left and how badly that little had been used by those who had looked upon the American land as a commodity to be appropriated or a resource to be stripped and gutted—without a thought for the future, without notable governmental interference, and all in the name of progress and enterprise. Against all the weight of history and tradition, Muir, and those who believed as he believed, gathered strength for a struggle whose resolution we have yet to see.

Probably the greatest devastation of the American land had taken place in its forests where cattlemen, sheepmen, and timber men combined to cripple millions of acres of watersheds—the "fountains of life," as Muir called them—the livestock men by overgrazing the high summer ranges of the mountains, and the timber men by "clear-cutting" a full century before the term came into general use. Neither had much to fear from government supervision. The General Land Office, the agency assigned the task of overseeing the use of the American public domain, was throughout its existence underfunded, understaffed, and thoroughly susceptible to political influence, and the laws regulating the use and disposal of land were so easily corrupted or circumvented that they might as well never have existed.

A particularly telling example was the Timber and Stone Act of 1878. This act applied only to those lands in California, Nevada, Oregon, and Washington that were "unfit for cultivation" and "valuable chiefly for timber and stone," and allowed any citizen or first-paper alien to claim and buy 160 acres of timberland for $2.50 an acre. Historian Ray Allen Billington has described what followed: "Company agents rounded up gangs of alien seamen in waterfront boarding houses, marched them to the courthouse to file their first papers, then to the land office to claim their quarter section, then to a notary public to sign over their deeds to the corporation, and back to the boarding houses to be paid off. Fifty dollars was the usual fee, although the amount soon fell to $5 or $10 and eventually to a glass of beer." The public domain was up for grabs, and the resulting timber-stripping and overgrazing was busily reducing much of the West to a bleak, corrugated, eroded wasteland.

California was by no means exempt from all this, nor was John Muir a stranger to it. In 1868 and 1869, he had already calculated the damage inflicted by "hooved locusts," and throughout the first years of his Sierra Nevada wanderings kept a weather eye out for similar destruction. "It is almost impossible," he wrote in his journal in September 1873, "to conceive of a devastation more universal than is produced among the plants of the Sierra by sheep. . . . The grass is eaten close and trodden until it resembles a corral, although the toughness of the sod preserves the roots from destruction. But where the soil is not preserved by a strong elastic sod, it is cut up and beaten to loose dust and every herbaceous plant is killed. Trees and bushes escape, but they appear to stand in a desert. . . . Nine-tenths of the whole surface of the Sierra has been swept by the scourge. It demands legislative interference."

Two years later, after witnessing logging operations among the sugar pines and sequoias of the southern Sierra, he was driven to philosophy: "I often wonder what man will do with the mountains— that is, with their utilizable, destructible garments. Will he cut down all the trees to make ships and houses? If so, what will be the final and far upshot? Will human destructions like those of Nature—fire and flood and avalanche—work out a higher good, a finer beauty? Will a better civilization come in accord with obvious nature, and all this wild beauty be set to human poetry and song? Another universal outpouring of lava, or the coming of a glacial period, could scarce wipe out the flowers and shrubs more effectually than do the sheep. And what then is coming? What is the human part of the mountains' destiny?"

Most tragic to Muir, of course, was the damage to the Yosemite and its environs —not just the valley floor, but the high grasslands above it, particularly those of the Tuolumne Meadows. These wider regions were still federal land; they had not been included in the Yosemite Park grant to the state of California in 1864, and they remained quite as helpless and unprotected as any forest land in the West. As early as 1878, he had begun talking up the idea of persuading the federal government to enlarge its original grant to include these lands, and in 1880 and 1881 had helped to shape legislation to that effect for introduction into Congress by California senator John F. Miller. The bill had died in committee, and for the next several years, caught up in the endless grind of work on the Alhambra ranch, he had been unable to make further efforts in that direction.

But there was a revolution brewing in these years, both in and out of government. At or near the head of it was Robert Underwood Johnson, associate editor of *Century* magazine, the successor to the old *Scribner's Monthly* in which many of Muir's articles of the 1870s had appeared. In the spring of 1889, Johnson arrived in California and immediately contacted Muir, hoping to get him to begin contributing to *Century*. Muir took him to the mountains, unsurprisingly, and while there showed Johnson some of the havoc wreaked by saws and hooves in the greater Yosemite region. The editor was deeply moved, and urged Muir to write two articles for *Century*, one pointing out the destruction and the other advocating the creation of a national park from these lands. Muir was skeptical. He had no illusions about the stewardship of the state, which the abuse of the Yosemite Valley floor had demonstrated was a disaster, but he doubted very much that the people of California cared enough to support such a park. Johnson pointed out that these lands did not merely belong to the people of California but to all of the people of the nation, and it would be all the people who would make a park.

Muir agreed to do the articles, and by the following summer had finished them: "Treasures of the Yosemite" and "Features of the Proposed Yosemite National Park," the first two in a long series of articles that would flow out of the cluttered workroom of the Alhambra Valley house over the next fifteen years. They were published immediately in successive issues of *Century*, and Johnson, pulling eastern strings and bending eastern ears, inspired the introduction of a Yosemite National Park Bill in Congress. It was passed, and on October 1, 1890, President Benjamin Harrison signed it into law; shortly thereafter federal troops were dispatched to the new park (until the formation of the National Park Service in 1916, the United States Army was charged with administering the nation's parks).

During their meeting in the summer of 1889, Johnson had urged Muir to "start an association for preserving California's monuments and natural wonders—or at least Yosemite," and over the next two years Muir had discussed the idea with his friends. Finally, on May 28, 1892, Muir and a group of mountaineers and conservationists met in the San Francisco office of attorney Warren Olney and put together an organization called the Sierra Club, whose articles of incorporation declared its purposes to be "to explore, enjoy, and render accessible the mountain regions of the Pacific Coast; to publish authentic information concerning them; to enlist the support and cooperation of the people and the government in preserving the forests and other natural features of the Sierra Nevada Mountains." Muir was elected president of the club and would hold that post until his death.

From the beginning, Muir had conceived the Sierra Club as a *tool*, not merely a gathering of convivial spirits, and almost immediately the young organization found it necessary to exercise the final clause in its articles of incorporation, for in that same year the so-called Caminetti Bill was introduced into Congress. This splendid measure would have gutted the newly-created Yosemite National Park by exempting some three hundred mining claims and large blocs of land desired by stockmen and timber men. After a two-year campaign of letter-writing, speech-making, and publicizing the conflict in newspaper articles, Muir and the club managed to have the bill defeated permanently in 1894.

Then there was the matter of the Yosemite Valley itself, which the state administered loosely, to say the least. Muir initiated a campaign to have the original grant returned to the federal government for inclusion in the national park that surrounded it; this crusade would take more than ten years. Throughout the early 1890s Muir, speaking for, through, and with the other club members, encouraged the establishment of forest reserves under the provisions of the Forest Reserve Act of 1891, which authorized the president to withdraw from entry, through any of the public land laws, any forest or watershed his Interior Department recommended for protection. Between 1891 and 1893, President Harrison created fifteen such reservations, several in the Sierra Nevada, and we may assume that Muir had some influence in the choices made.

In 1893, Muir took a vacation from all such concerns by setting off on a trip to Europe—specifically to Scotland where he wanted to revisit his boyhood home. In New York he was captured by Robert Underwood Johnson and carted around to clubs and dinners and champagne breakfasts, just as in his first days in San Francisco and Oakland so many years before. He had mellowed by now, however, and he truly enjoyed the experience (it did not hurt that his reputation had preceded him and that he was treated with enormous respect, even awe, by such as Mark Twain, Thomas Bailey Aldrich, Nikola Tesla,

Rudyard Kipling, Charles Dudley Warner, George W. Cable, and John Burroughs). Before taking the ship to Liverpool, he made a quick journey up to New England to visit the graves of Emerson and Thoreau and to hike around the shores of Walden Pond. ("No wonder Thoreau lived here two years," he wrote to his wife. "I could have enjoyed living here two hundred years or two thousand.")

On June 26 he left for England, and for the next three months he walked, horse-backed, and sailed around and through Scotland, England, Ireland, Norway, and Switzerland, marveling at the great glacial fjords of the North Sea countries, considering and rejecting a climb of the Matterhorn, luxuriating in the lushness of England's Lake District, and reminiscing with cousins and old schoolmates in Dunbar, which he found so little changed from the days of his youth that it seemed he had never left.

Back home in October, he plunged into the completion of his first book, *The Mountains of California*, a collection of his mountain articles plus some new material. It was published in the fall of 1894 by the Century Company, and Muir could now know a writer's inexpressible pleasure at seeing his words given the permanence of binding. The book was not a best seller in the modern sense of the term, but it was a definite success; it went into a second printing almost immediately and added a good measure to his influence in the world. He would need the extra clout, for the forest reservation battle was soon warming up again.

In 1896, during the last year of the second administration of President Grover Cleveland, the Secretary of the Interior requested the National Academy of Sciences to investigate the "necessity of a radical change in the existing policy with reference to the disposal of and preservation of the forests upon the public domain. . . ." The Academy accommodated the Secretary by sending a committee on a swing through the forested West from July to October. Muir was invited to join the committee on an unofficial basis and did so, accompanying its members (among whom was a young forester by the name of Gifford Pinchot) from the Black Hills of South Dakota, through the Cascades, the northern Sierra, and Southern California to the Grand Canyon. Upon its return to Washington, the committee began preparing a report among whose recommendations was the addition of several more forest reserves. Although the report would not become official until its publication more than six months later, Cleveland implemented it as one of the last acts of his administration. On Washington's Birthday, 1897, he proclaimed the addition of 21 million acres to the forest system in thirteen individual reserves from the Cascades to the Black Hills of South Dakota.

The reaction of the industry-dominated western press was predictably violent. "A Menace to the Interests of the Western States," headlined the *Denver Republican*, and the editor of the *San Francisco Chronicle* averred that the withdrawals had been made "for no other reason than that the wiseacres of the National Academy of Sciences, who nominated the amiable theorists who reported a scheme of forest reservation for the West, believed that what would be well for one part of the country would be the best for all."

This in turn inspired an answer from the hot pen of Muir in the *Atlantic Monthly*, one of the most effective conservation statements he ever wrote: "The outcries we hear against forest reservations come mostly from thieves who are wealthy and steal timber by wholesale. They have so long been allowed to steal and destroy in peace that any impediment to forest robbery is denounced as a cruel and irreligious interference with 'vested rights,' likely to endanger the repose of all ungodly welfare. . . . Any fool can destroy trees. They cannot run away; and if they could, they would be hunted down as long as fun or a dollar could be got out of their bark hides, branching horns, or magnificent bole backbones. Few that fell trees plant them; nor would planting avail much towards getting back anything like the noble primeval forests. During a man's life only saplings can be grown, in the place of the old trees—tens of centuries old—that have been destroyed. It took more than three thousand years to make some of the trees that are still standing in perfect strength and beauty, waving and singing in the mighty forests of the Sierra. Through all the wonderful, eventful centuries since Christ's time—and long before that—God has cared for these trees, saved them from drought, disease, avalanches, and a thousand straining, leveling tempests and floods; but He cannot save them from fools—only Uncle Sam can do that."

In early 1898 a movement was afoot in Congress to introduce legislation that would repeal the president's power to make forest reservations and eliminate those already made. The proposal got through the Senate but failed in the House, and at least one conservationist,

C. S. Sargent, who had headed up the 1896 investigating committee, was willing to lay a good deal of the credit at Muir's door: "You have evidently been putting in some good work," Sargent wrote to Muir. "On Saturday all the members of the Public Lands Committee of the House agreed to oppose the Senate amendment wiping out the reservations." A skirmish, and an important one, had been won. Yet Muir was learning what two generations of conservationists after him would learn: the struggle to protect and preserve the land was a war that had no ending, only armed truces. "There are clarifications as well as discouragements in the study of history," Wallace Stegner has written. "It demonstrates with precision who the adversaries are. Always are." Muir's would be with him until he died.

"Evenin' Brings a Hame..."

In 1898, Muir was sixty years old, but the wanderlust was as strong in him now as it had been in his youth. It was a matter of health, one is tempted to guess, as much as anything else. Travel invigorated him quite as much as it was inclined to weaken other people his age, and staying tucked away in the Alhambra Valley, dozing by a fire or quietly shuffling through memories, held no appeal for him. In fact, too long in the haven of home tended to sicken him even when working, and in the two years of writing and legislating since his European trip he had once again become shadowy. A persistent cold haunted him, and the old rasping cough gave him constant misery. He therefore prescribed for himself his usual remedy: travel.

In September 1898, he left for an excursion through the American South, revisiting some of the scenes of Kentucky, Tennessee, South Carolina, Georgia, and Florida which he had encountered during his thousand-mile walk to the Gulf thirty years before—including looking up old Mrs. Hodgson, the only remaining member of the family that had nursed him through malaria at Cedar Key.

He had only just returned from this trip when he was off again for Alaska, in whose climate he was convinced no microbe could survive. This time it was with the Harriman Expedition ship, the *George W. Elder*, a vessel owned by Edward H. Harriman, president of the Union Pacific Railroad (and in a few years of the Southern Pacific as well). The ship was splendidly fitted out with an impressive array of scientific instruments, complete with the scientists that went with them, including Henry Gannett, chief geographer of the U. S. Geological Survey, C. Hart Merriam, chief of the U. S. Biological Survey, William Ritter, a marine biologist from the University of California, Muir himself, and fellow Scotsman and naturalist John Burroughs. With Muir guiding them all on land excursions (and occasionally acting as pilot for the ship itself), the 126 members of the expedition got a quick but intensive tour of the Alaskan coast—from Portland to Sitka, Glacier Bay, Disenchantment Bay, Yakutat Bay, Prince William Sound, and Kodiak Island, then a stormy introduction to the Bering Sea through the Unimak Pass, touching at the Pribilof Islands, Plover Bay on the Siberian coast, and Saint Lawrence Island, just south of the Bering Strait, before heading back to the United States. It was a trip that John Burroughs never forgot. At Kodiak Island he had wanted to remain behind, fearing for his tender stomach on the Bering Sea. Muir browbeat him out of it, claiming that the sea was a very mirror of smoothness. On the way to the Pribilofs, while he lay in his bed, rolling with the storm-buffeted ship, the green-gilled Burroughs penned a grouchy poem that included a classic couplet:

> Where every prospect pleases,
> And only Muir is vile.

Ensconced on the ranch again, bubbling with the sweet energy given him by the Alaska venture, Muir finished his second book, *Our National Parks*, and saw it published in the early fall of 1901. He also saw, along with the rest of the nation, the arrival of Theodore Roosevelt to the presidency in September of that year, after an assassin's bullet dispatched William McKinley. New York patrician by birth, western cowboy by avocation, and mover-and-shaker by instinct, Roosevelt proved to be a vigorous conservationist, and his administration, bold, blustery, self-consciously (and often self-righteously) progressive, put teeth in the movement for resource management and land reform. One of the first whose advice he sought was Muir.

"The President is heartily with us in the matter of preserving the forests and keeping out the sheep," C. Hart Merriam wrote Muir in October. "He wants to know the facts . . . from men like yourself who are not connected with the Government service and at the same time are known and esteemed by the people." Muir was quick to give the president the facts as he saw them, including not only an outline of the destruction he had seen in the forests of the Pacific slope and other parts of the West, but the recommendation that the miniscule Forestry Department, organized in 1898 with young Gifford Pinchot at its head, be renamed the Bureau of Forestry and moved out of the Department of the Interior to the Department of Agriculture, which Muir felt was better equipped to regulate forest use. The idea did not originate with Muir, and Roosevelt certainly had heard the same proposal from a number of sources by then, but Muir's was a voice to be reckoned with. In any case, in his first annual message to Congress on December 3, 1901, Roosevelt declared that "the forest and water problems are perhaps the most vital internal questions of the United States at the present time," and went on to advocate the vigorous protection of forest reserves from the onslaught of livestock, particularly sheep—and the creation of a Bureau of Forestry under the Department of Agriculture (this was in fact done in 1905, although the agency was named the United States Forest Service).

Eighteen months later Muir had the opportunity to exercise his influence more directly. Early in 1903 he heard from Robert Underwood Johnson that Roosevelt was planning to visit California in the spring and that he had expressed the specific desire to have Muir shepherd him around Yosemite. That information was later confirmed by similar assurances from Chester Rowell, one of the leaders of the progressive Lincoln-Roosevelt League of California, and Benjamin Ide Wheeler, president of the University of California. But Muir had already made plans to begin a tour of forest lands in Russia, Manchuria, and Japan with Charles S. Sargent, chairman of the National Forestry Commission of 1896, in May, the month the president was expected to arrive. A personal letter from Roosevelt, however, tipped the balance: "I do not want anyone with me but you, and I want to drop politics absolutely for four days, and just be out in the open with you."

One did not—one does not—ignore personal requests by the president of the United States, and besides, as Muir wrote to Sargent, explaining that he would have to postpone the date of their sailing, "I might be able to *do some forest good* in freely talking around the campfire." Roosevelt arrived in San Francisco on May 15. They spent their first night together in front of a campfire in the Mariposa Grove of Big Trees, their second night in a meadow just behind Glacier Point above the Yosemite Valley, and the third night in Bridalveil Meadow on the valley floor. As might be expected, Roosevelt at one point announced, "Now this is bully!" and Muir did in fact take advantage of the situation to do "some forest good," filling Roosevelt's ear with a steady litany of persuasion. He found a ready listener, and if Roosevelt was not a champion of forest preservation when he arrived in California, he most certainly was when he later came down out of the mountains with Muir.

Stopping in Sacramento on his way back east, the president gave an impromptu address whose text might as well have been lifted from the works of John Muir: "I have just come from a four days' rest in Yosemite, and I wish to say a word to you here . . . about certain of your great natural resources, your forests. . . . As regards some of the trees, I want them preserved because they are the only things of their kind in the world. Lying out at night under those giant sequoias was lying in a temple built by no hand of man, a temple grander than any human architect could by any possibility build, and I hope for the preservation of the groves of giant trees simply because it would be a shame to our civilization to let them disappear. They are monuments in themselves. I ask for the preservation of other forests on the grounds of wise and far-sighted economic policy. I do not ask that lumbering be stopped . . . only that the forests be so used that not only shall we here, this generation, get the benefit for the next few years, but that our children and our children's children shall get the benefit. . . . We are not building this country of ours for a day. It is to last through the ages." At the time of his address, there were a little over 46 million acres of forest land in reserves; by the time he left office in 1909, Roosevelt had added another 148 million.

His duty to the trees done for the moment, Muir left for the trip with Sargent. In all respects it was the single most far-reaching and remarkable of all the journeys of his life. It took him to London, Paris, Berlin, Moscow, Saint Petersburg (Leningrad), Sevastopol, Vladivostok, Shanghai, Calcutta, Darjeeling, Simla, Bombay, Cairo, Melbourne, Sydney, Auckland (New Zealand), Manila, Canton, Tokyo,

Nagasaki, and Yokohama—a "most monstrous dose of civilization" he called these urban stops. More to his taste and his desire were the landscapes he had seen: the Lindula Forest of Finland, the glaciers of the Caucasus Mountains, the valleys of the Ural and the Volga, the glacial fjords of the Korean coast, the deodar forests of India, the Himalayas touched by the morning sun, the Libyan desert, the First Cataract of the Nile River, the "forest primeval" seventy miles inland from Melbourne, as well as the Blue Mountains and casuarina forests near Sydney, the Mueller Glacier of Mount Cook in New Zealand, the jungles of the Philippines, the great cone of Fujiyama rising like an Olympus on the big island of Honshu, Japan. As in his youth (he was now sixty-five years of age), he collected and pressed hundreds of botanical specimens, lifting his personal collection to the level of one of the most comprehensive private collections in the world. During much of the earlier part of the trip, beset by too many months spent in European cities, he had been very ill, at one point weighing only 90 pounds, but by the time he arrived at the docks in San Francisco a little over a year from the time of his departure, he was as brown and sturdy as a slab of polished Philippine mahogany—and weighed 148 pounds, the most he had ever weighed in his entire life.

He would need the newborn health, for the question of the future of the Yosemite Valley, which had been quietly bubbling for more than ten years, would come to a full, rolling boil in the next few months. Muir, of course, had been consistently working during this time to have the state park returned to the federal government for inclusion within the larger national park, and generally speaking, so had the Sierra Club. Yet this was an especially emotional issue; many people in California felt that giving up the park would be demeaning to the state, and among these were some members of the club itself, as suggested in an 1897 letter which Muir wrote to Warren Olney: "I don't see that one or two objectors should have the right to kill all action of the Club in this or any other matter rightly belonging to it. Professor Davidson's objection is also held by Professor LeConte, or was, but how they can consistently sing praise to the Federal Government in the management of the National Parks, and at the same time regard the same management of Yosemite as degrading to the State, I can't see. . . . And as to our Secretary's objection, it seemed to me merely political, and if the Sierra Club is to be run by politicians, the sooner mountaineers get out of it the better." Steady campaigning over the years had calmed most of the opposition in the club, however, and when in January 1905, Muir and the club's then secretary, William E. Colby, journeyed to Sacramento to begin a season of lobbying, they had behind them the great majority of the club's membership.

The matter in question was a bill in the state legislature to offer the state park to the government, and Muir and Colby bent their energies toward its passage. "I am now an experienced lobbyist," Muir wrote to Robert Underwood Johnson some time later. "My political education is complete. Have attended Legislature, made speeches, explained, exhorted, persuaded every mother's son of the legislators, newspaper reporters, and everybody else who would listen to me."

The effort was successful, but only just; the recession bill passed the assembly by a startling vote of 45 to 20, but got through the senate by only one vote, and it might not have passed even by that thin margin if Muir had not called upon his friend, Edward H. Harriman, to put the weight of the Southern Pacific's political machine behind the project. Muir, the poet and wilderness philosopher, the man who took no small pleasure in presenting himself as the archetypal unworldly sort, was capable of astonishing flights of hard-nosed political realism. He held no brief for the Southern Pacific's heavy—in fact, corrupt—hand on California's political and economic life, but he demonstrated himself quite willing to use it for his own ends. What is more, when opposition to acceptance of the Yosemite recession was expressed in Congress, he called upon Harriman again—with similarly successful results. The grant was accepted by the government of the United States, and never again would the floor of the Yosemite valley echo to the dull thud of the hooves of sheep and cattle. "Yes, my dear Johnson," he wrote to the *Century*'s editor, "sound the loud timbrel and let every Yosemite tree and stream rejoice!"

In personal terms the successful fight to have the Yosemite Valley included in the National Park was perhaps Muir's greatest triumph; for more than thirty years the valley had been the talisman of his soul, had healed him in his periods of depression and exhaustion, had enlarged and in many ways defined his life, and now he could feel that he had adequately returned the love he had found there. The moment, however, was the last one of undiluted happiness that he would know. Even as he

John Muir, wild man of the mountains—a self-portrait from a letter of February 23, 1887.

was fighting the legislative battle, his daughter Helen was stricken with pneumonia and was a long time recovering. In May, Muir took her to Arizona to set up a life for her in the clear desert air where her lungs might heal. He was still there on June 24, when he received a telegram telling him that his wife was desperately ill. He hurried back to the Alhambra Valley to be at her side; there was no help to be had, however, for she had lung cancer and was dead on August 6. Muir buried her on the ranch with her parents and dully went about the business of his life.

He did not fully recover from the loss of his wife for some three years, and at that point was presented with yet another agony, one that would exhaust his mind and heart and bring him as close to despair and bitterness as anything in his life.

As early as 1890, the city officials of San Francisco had begun glancing at the Sierra Nevada as a potential source of water for the fast-growing city. An early engineering study had pointed out the advantages —most of them economical—of a reservoir site in the Hetch Hetchy gorge of the Tuolumne River. That this valley was within the boundaries of Yosemite National Park and that many people, at the head of whom was Muir himself, considered it second in beauty only to Yosemite, was not a consideration in the minds of either engineers or city officials. In 1901, Mayor James D. Phelan petitioned the Department of the Interior for permission to use the valley as a reservoir site. He was turned down, and over the next several years each succeeding petition was treated similarly, largely because of pressures against the idea by conservationists. But in 1908, Interior Secretary James Garfield granted the petition. "The City," he noted, "would have one of the finest and purest water supplies in the world; the irrigable land in the Tuolumne and San Joaquin valleys [there was no irrigable land in the Tuolumne Valley; there was, in fact, *no* Tuolumne Valley] would be helped out by the use of the excess stored water and by using the electrical power not needed by the City for municipal purposes, to pump subterranean water for the irrigation of additional areas; the City would have a cheap and bountiful supply of electrical energy for pumping its water supply and lighting the City and its municipal buildings."

To this and all other arguments John Muir had one answer, the same as that given in a letter to Roosevelt in 1908: "I am heartily in favor of a Sierra or even a Tuol-umne water supply for San Francisco, but all the water required can be obtained from sources outside the Park, leaving the twin valleys, Hetch-Hetchy and Yosemite, to the use they were intended for when the Park was established. . . . The few promoters of the present scheme are not unknown around the boundaries of the Park, for some of them have been trying to break through for years. However able they may be as capitalists, engineers, lawyers, or even philanthropists, none of the statements they have made descriptive of Hetch-Hetchy dammed or undammed is true, but they all show forth the proud sort of confidence that comes of a good, sound, substantial, irrefragable ignorance. For example, the capitalist Mr. James D. Phelan says, 'There are a thousand places in the Sierra equally as beautiful as Hetch-Hetchy: it is inaccessible nine months of the year, and is an unlivable place the other three months because of mosquitoes.' On the contrary, there is not another of its kind in all the Park excepting Yosemite. It is accessible all the year, and is not more mosquitoful than Yosemite. 'The conversion of Hetch-Hetchy into a reservoir will simply mean a lake instead of a meadow.' But Hetch-Hetchy is not a meadow: it is a Yosemite Valley. . . . These sacred mountain temples are the holiest ground that the heart of man has consecrated, and it behooves us all faithfully to do our part in seeing that our wild mountain parks are passed on unspoiled to those who come after us, for they are national properties in which every man has a right and interest."

Essentially, the battle lines were drawn between two kinds of conservation: the purely utilitarian faction, which steadfastly believed that conservation should be for *use*, not merely beauty; and the faction represented by Muir and the Sierra Club, which was willing to entertain the idea of use, but not at the sacrifice of values that could not be measured in money. Even then it was an old battle. It is an old battle still. By dint of almost constant effort, the Muir faction managed to keep Congress from approving Garfield's permit through the rest of the Roosevelt administration and on through the administration of William H. Taft. By 1911 what appeared to be an impasse had been reached.

Muir had not confined himself to the Hetch Hetchy fight during these years. He had written *Stickeen*, published in 1909, and *My First Summer in the Sierra*, published in 1911, and had revised and enlarged *The Mountains of California*, the new edition coming out also in 1911.

And in that year he finally satisfied an urge that had first come to him in the middle of the 1860s: he traveled to South America, in spite of objections from his doctor, his friends, and his daughters, refusing to take into consideration the fact that he was then seventy-three years old. "The world's big," he said, "and I want to have a look at it before it gets dark." And so he did, steaming up to the headwaters of the Amazon and back, then crossing the South American continent by train to Chile, climbing up into the slopes of the Andes and spending a night beneath a grove of monkey puzzle trees. Not satisfied with having achieved this forty-four-year-old ambition, he then sailed for South Africa, where he ventured into the jungle to put his hands on a baobab tree, another old ambition.

He returned early in 1912 quite as fat and healthy as he always did from trips that everyone else believed would kill him. He began organizing his notes for a book he would call *Travels in Alaska* and was soon plunged into the "everlasting" Hetch Hetchy fight again, as the election of Woodrow Wilson in November 1912 brought in a new secretary of the interior, Franklin K. Lane, a former city attorney of San Francisco and long an advocate of the Hetch Hetchy reservoir. Lane put his office behind efforts to get legislation passed allowing the city to go ahead, and in September 1913, the enabling bill was passed by the House, 183 to 43. Led by William E. Colby, secretary of the Sierra Club, Muir's forces made a last-ditch stand in the Senate throughout November, but to no avail. The bill was passed and sent to President Wilson, who signed it into law.

Hetch Hetchy was lost, but not even to his closest friends did Muir reveal the degree to which his soul had been shattered by what he saw as a mindless capitulation to the insensate demands of urban growth and "moneyed interests." Everything his life had meant had been challenged and defeated, and he found little solace in all his other accomplishments—the creation, not only of Yosemite National Park, but of Grand Canyon National Monument and the Petrified Forest National Monument (both of which he had persuaded Theodore Roosevelt to establish), as well as the reservation of millions of acres of forest land throughout the West. Still, he would not, could not, embrace cynicism and despair, not completely. "The destruction of the charming groves and gardens, the finest in all California," he wrote to William E. Colby, "goes to my heart. But in spite of Satan & Co. some sort of compensation must surely come out of this dark damn-dam-damnation."

If there was to be compensation, Muir would not live to see it. "I'm somewhat run down for want of exercise, and exhausting work and worry," he wrote his daughter Helen shortly after the Hetch Hetchy defeat. He was, in fact, chronically ill; the old cough was back, and this time it simply would not go away. Stubbornly, he stayed at his desk for twelve, fourteen, sixteen hours a day working on *Travels in Alaska*, quite possibly knowing that it would be his last book.

By December 1914, the basic manuscript was complete, needing only minor revisions here and there, and he decided to take it with him on a visit to Helen, now living with her husband and children in Daggett in the Mojave Desert of Southern California. Weak, and thin to the point of emaciation, he was dropped in the winter desert from the train at half past two in the morning. By the following evening, his persistent cold had developed into pneumonia, and he was rushed to the California Hospital in Los Angeles. He revived briefly while there, and seemed to be on the way to recovery, but on the morning of December 24, his nurse stepped in to check on him and found him dead, the manuscript pages of his book spread on the coverlet around him.

Forty-seven years before, while camped out among the gray tombs of the Bonaventure graveyard outside Savannah, Georgia, a younger Muir had essayed some notions about death. "But let children walk with Nature," he had scribbled in his journal, "let them see the beautiful blendings and communions of death and life, their joyous inseparable unity, as taught in woods and meadows, plains and mountains and streams of our blessed star, and they will learn that death is stingless indeed, and as beautiful as life, and that the grave has no victory, for it never fights." And as the friends and relatives of his life had slipped away through the years, Muir had often quoted the old Scotch saying, "Evenin' brings a hame."

On Christmas Eve, 1914, at the age of seventy-six, John Muir found a home in the unity of life and death.

The Third Dialogue

Yosemite

*I*t is difficult to believe this valley. It is something to be felt, to be dreamed of, to be experienced, but not to be believed, something as unreal as a dream, an exercise of the imagination. It is too large a beauty to be fully embraced by the human mind. Perhaps if you, like the old man, had lived ten years of your life here, wandering its floor and climbing its walls, searching out all the secrets of the forces that had made it, gathering its plants, touching its trees, learning the conversation of its storms and seasons, perhaps then you could accept it. But you have not done that. Almost no one but the old man ever has.

However, you know its names well enough: Bridalveil Fall, Cascade Fall, Vernal Fall, Nevada Fall, Yosemite Fall, upper and lower; Arch Rock, Pulpit Rock, Inspiration Point, Rocky Point, Clouds' Rest, El Capitan, Half Dome, North Dome, Glacier Point, Royal Arches, Washington Column; Merced River, Mirror Lake. You are standing now on Sunnyside Bench on the north wall of the valley, not far from lower Yosemite Fall and about five hundred feet above the valley floor. You have climbed here with the old man up a reasonably easy trail, though your mind has filled with images of plunging death and your city-trained body has objected every step of the way.

The old man has not been sympathetic. "Hurry, lad, hurry!" he has urged you while scrambling up the rocks like a mountain goat, casting impatient glances back at you. "It's worth dying to see this." You doubt it, but you follow him never-theless. Resting now on the bench, surrounded by ferns and flowers and wild vines, with groves of oak and pine behind you and the whole length of the valley before you, you are tempted to believe him. A little to the west of where you are, lower Yosemite Fall spurts out over the lip of a cliff and tumbles down to the floor of the valley, its distant rumbling a steady mutter that fills the wind, its mist rising into the air above it like fog.

133

It is late afternoon in the early fall, and the old man has brought you up here because he has sniffed out an approaching storm, though all you can see are a few scattered clouds moving up toward the valley from the southwest. While you wait for something to happen, watching the shadows lengthening across the valley floor as the sun slips down the western sky, you tell the old man of a critic of mountain climbing you once read, whose conviction was that those who climb mountains are, in fact, insane, that God did not put mountains on the earth to satisfy the egos of those who would like to conquer them.

The old man laughs his barking laugh. "Aye, lad, if it's put that way, I canna but agree. God didna put the mountains there to satisfy anything in man. They have their own reason for being, and like the great sequoia, it has naught to do with man. But yeer birkie confused the issue."

"What do you mean?"

"He assumed that a man climbs a mountain to conquer it, to stand in triumph upon it."

"Well, doesn't he? Isn't that why he does it? Why else?"

"For some that is the reason, I'll agree. But not for all. Most sairly not for me."

"What, then?"

The old man rubs a finger up against his nose, a habit you have noticed he practices whenever he has to explain something he is not sure you will understand. "Weel, I'm not certain I can make it clear to ye. What I wanted above all else was to become part of these mountains, to be accepted as one with them. I didna see them as enemies who had thrown up obstacles and redoubts to prevent my advance. I saw them as friends who offered paths for me to follow, if I could but see them. And the paths were always there, lad, in every cliff and overhang and chimney, on every ridge and slope, the way was shown, always. The mountains welcome those who will accept them for what they are. Those who approach them in any other way demean both themselves and the mountains." The old man walked to the edge of the bench. "Come here, lad, this is what we came to see."

You join him and marvel at the perception of the man who has brought you here. The scattered clouds you had noticed earlier have gathered together now, rolling and boiling in a heavy yellow-black mass on the other side of the valley. The wind has picked up, whipping cold drafts of its breath against you. Beneath the mountain of clouds you can see strands of rain begin to touch down on the swelling crest of Half Dome. The pine forests on the opposite slope are soon shrouded in mist, which lies over them like a blanket drawn up over the face of a dead man. Flashes of lightning crackle down, editorial comments from God. It is a spectacular show, and it is a long time before you notice that the storm has moved across the distance between the two walls of Yosemite, filling the valley floor with clouds, filling the sky above you with their moving, cottony presence.

"This is where it began for you, isn't it?" you ask.

The old man shakes his head slowly, his gaze on the sky. "No, not really. It began

a long time before that—aye, perhaps as long before as my childhood in Dunbar,
when I heard my first bird singing joy to the morning. Or when I found a nest
of baby mice in a haystack, no bigger than shrimp and just as pink, new with life.
But ye're right, in a way. It was here, in this valley, in these mountains, that
my life took on purpose, almost as if the guid God himself had been saving it for me—
or me for it."

"We haven't done as well by this valley as we might have."

"No, no, ye haven't. But, God help me, I can take some of the blame for that.
When they first wanted to bring automobiles into the valley, I said let them—let those
snorting beasts mix their fumes with the smell of the pines. It wouldn't make any
difference, I said." He rubs the back of his neck with a hand. "Jimmie Bryce
knew better."

"Jimmie Bryce?"

"James Bryce, British ambassador to the United States when I knew him. He was
a Scotsman, too, and a lover of the valley, and it sorrows me to know that he saw
farther into the future than I could. It was in 1912 or 1913 that he said it: 'If
Adam had known what harm the serpent was going to work, he would have tried
to prevent him from finding lodgment in Eden; and if you were to realize what
the result of the automobile will be in that wonderful, that incomparable valley, you
will keep it out.' Aye, he knew and I didn't."

"We've learned since, I think—I hope."

"'Tis not enough to hope. Ye have to work for it—I learned that much. And if ye
don't," he adds, spreading his arms in a symbolic embrace, "if ye canna preserve
the oldest and best of all the parks, what is there left for the rest of yeer warl'?"

The clouds by now have towered over you and beyond you. It is as if you stood
at the base of a great black wave that was ready to break into foam and speed to death
on a beach lost in the mists of horizon. The wind is cold and heavy with moisture.
Soon rain splatters at your feet, great pounding drops that create little craters
in the earth. You are quickly wet, but the old man does not seem to notice your
discomfort. He stands in the middle of the storm, his face turned up into the force of
its rain, the look of a crazy man on his face. You tug at his sleeve, and slowly, slowly,
he turns to you.

"Isn't it time we left?" you ask.

"Leave? Great God, mon! Would ye be at home, dry and defrauded of all the
glory of this storm? Your soul would starve in the midst of abundance. Listen, lad,
listen to what the storm would teach you. You are part of this world, not something
that walks about in it without connection. You are one with everything in it—
rocks, flowers, trees, soil, storms, mountains. Do ye na see that that is what ye
must learn, all of ye? Ye're the best that the earth has produced, but ye've been pro-
duced by the earth, not separate from it. Ye're earthly beings, the highest of all
earthly beings, but ye're highest because all other forms of life have flowed into ye,
yeer being has flowed through all other forms and ye've taken parts of them with

ye, absorbing and assimilating portions of them into yourself. Ye're a being most richly divine because most richly terrestrial, just as a river becomes rich by flowing on through all its climes and rocks, through all its mountains and valleys, constantly taking parts of the earth with it. This storm is part of all that, part of what the earth has to give ye."

But you must leave, you say. You fear the darkness of the trail, the uncertainty of your return.

"Aye, go then. Leave me here."

You go back to the thin pathway and begin making your way down to the valley floor, to dryness and safety. Looking back, you can just barely see him outlined like a shadow against the curtain of rain. His face is still turned up into the falling water, as if he were standing beneath one of the great falls of the valley.

Goodbye, old man. They buried you on the Alhambra Valley ranch with your wife and her mother and father. It is where you wanted to be, but it would have been better to see your grave beneath one of the great trees you loved so much, your body's essence seeping into the ground, being appropriated by the tree's roots, sucked up and becoming part of the tree's branches, twigs, and leaves, expiring into the air, becoming a living part of the cycle of life and death whose meaning you carried in your mind and heart. That meaning is now ours. Let us remember it.

ABOVE: Young woodpecker, Sequoia National Park.　　　　　　　　OVERLEAF: Giant sequoias, Sequoia National Park.

"The clearest way into the Universe is through a forest wilderness."

Belding ground squirrel, Yosemite.

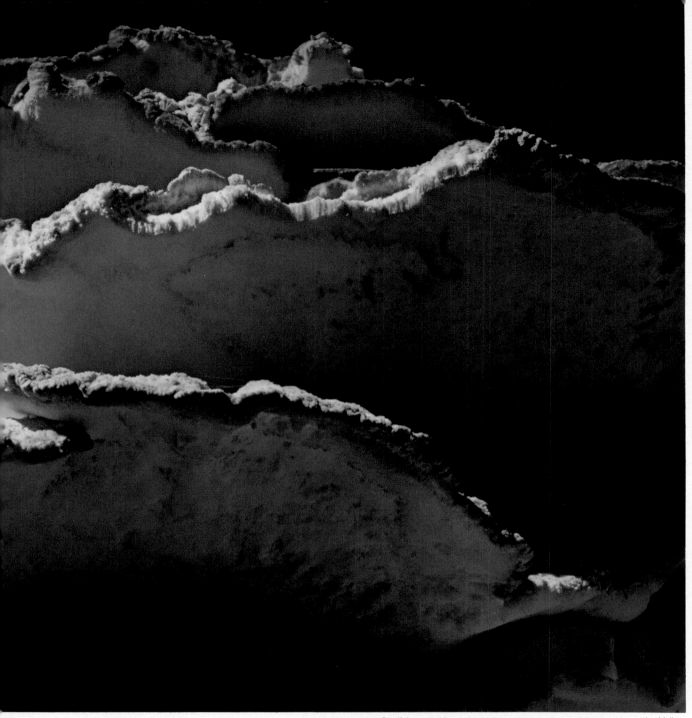

ABOVE: Shelf fungus, Yosemite Valley. OVERLEAF: Half Dome, Yosemite Valley.

"*Thus it appears that everything here is marching to music, and the harmonies are all so simple and young they are easily apprehended by those who will keep still and listen and look . . . .*"

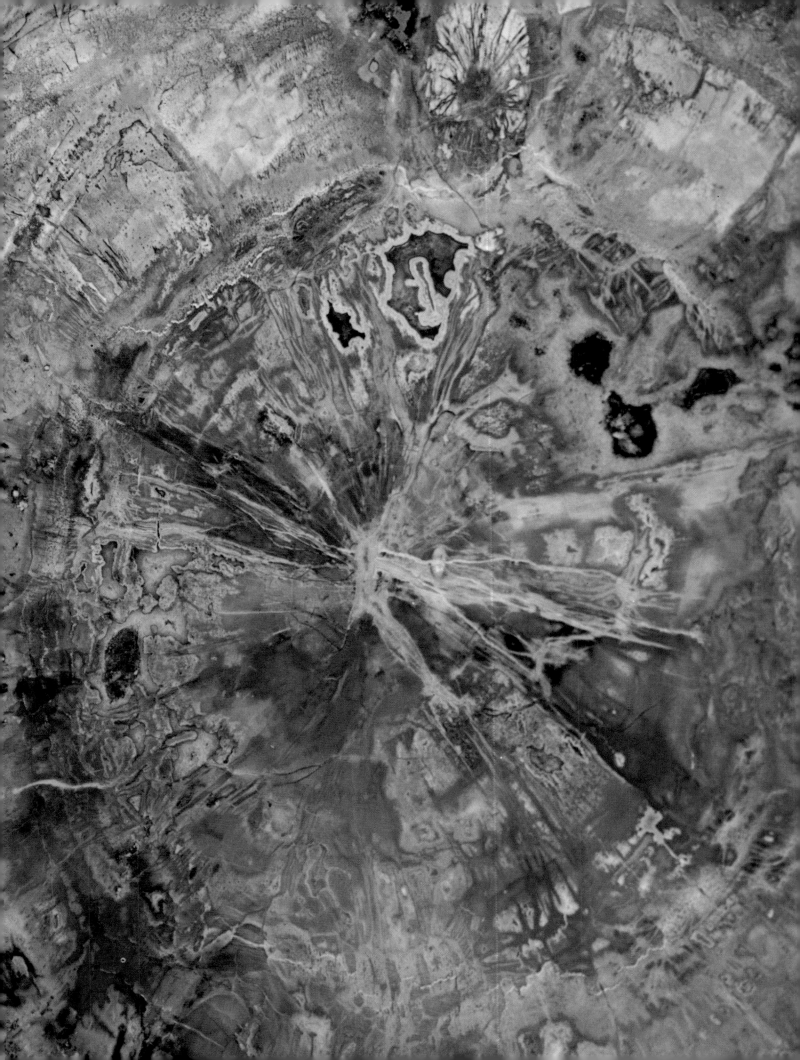

LEFT: Polished slice of petrified wood.   ABOVE: Petrified stumps, Petrified Forest National Park.   OVERLEAF: Grand Pacific Glacier, Glacier Bay.

"It was not like taking the veil. No solemn adjuration of the world.
I only went out for a walk and finally decided to stay till
sundown. For going out I found that I was really going in."

Waterwheel Falls, Yosemite.

View from Moro Rock, Sequoia National Park.

"This grand show is eternal. It is always sunrise somewhere; the dew is never all dried at once; a shower is forever falling; vapor is ever rising. Eternal sunrise, eternal sunset, eternal dawn and gloaming, on sea and continents and islands, each in its turn, as the round earth rolls."

OVERLEAF: Jeffrey pine, Sentinel Dome, Yosemite.

Photographic Notes

My observations on the photographs in this book can be broken down into two categories: what I can explain and what I can only hint at, the latter being by far the more important.

What I can explain is mostly technical. The photographs are all 35mm, and most of them were shot on Kodachrome II because it has virtually no grain. The camera I use is a Nikkormat, a single-lens reflex with a built-in light meter. I carry two of these in the field and a number of lenses: 20mm, 28mm, 35mm, 55mm macro, 105mm, and 200mm. Back in the car, I'll also have a 400mm and a 500mm, add a polarizing filter, a good tripod (Tiltall), a back-up light meter (Lunasix) in case the ones in the cameras give me trouble, and I'm ready to go. So much for what I can explain.

When I say I can only hint at the rest, it's not out of any desire to hide creative secrets. It's because most of my photography is done on an intuitive level and usually for reasons beyond the photograph itself.

Photography to me is not an end but a means to an end. The end is a life-style, an attitude, an approach to the world that is filled with both reverence and wonder. My photography helps me pursue this end. It allows me to travel, to steep myself in the thoughts of men like Muir, and to concentrate my vision on those aspects of nature that move me deeply.

I saw things while photographing for this book that were unspeakably beautiful. Time and again nature brought together light and line and shape in ways that made my heart dance and my mind rejoice. The photographs I took were only the remains of a banquet that was indescribable.

Nature spreads this banquet constantly, with no thought of whether anyone will actually attend. If I were receptive enough, perhaps I would see it in everything. But I can't, so photography is one of the tools I use to concentrate, to look deeply, to block out with the lens all that is extraneous and see that which is essential.

There's no magic inherent in the camera; it's just an aid. It can also be a handicap. How many times have I found myself at the end of a long assignment unable to see anything *except* through a lens—totally dead to the world except when I look through my camera. Enough! That's the time to put it away.

Or how many times have I been completely involved in the scene before me, transported by it to a place beyond expression, when my hand reaches instinctively into my shoulder bag and I place a camera between me and the experience. In both cases the camera has gotten in the way of the very kind of receptivity I want it to help me with.

The seeing is always more important than the photograph. When the photograph becomes an end in itself, then it will be time for me to stop. I make my living through photography, but it's what photography puts me in touch with that I'm really interested in. The money and kudos are important; the seeing is essential.

If some of the banquet I speak of comes through in my pictures, then I have succeeded. It's out there, believe me, beyond anything we can imagine. Muir saw it. It permeated both his life and his writing. He put it into words far better than I can when he said:

"I used to envy the father of our race, dwelling as he did in contact with the new-made fields and plants of Eden; but I do so no more, because I have discovered that I also live in 'creation's dawn.' The morning stars still sing together, and the world, not yet half made, becomes more beautiful every day."

—DEWITT JONES

Photographic Details

PAGE 1: A lone Jeffrey pine on Sentinel Dome, Yosemite, 28mm lens; Kodachrome II.

PAGES 2–3: An iceberg stranded in Muir Inlet, Glacier Bay, Alaska. These bergs break off the glaciers and float out to sea with the tide. The larger ones are usually beached several times before they reach the ocean. 105mm lens: Kodachrome II.

PAGES 4–5: The sun setting behind a petrified log in Petrified Forest National Park, Arizona. The foreground rocks are also petrified wood. 20mm lens; Kodachrome II.

PAGES 6–7: Sunrise over Yosemite Valley on a misty fall morning. Exposure is tricky when shooting into the sun, so I always bracket exposures in situations like this. 20mm lens; Kodachrome II.

PAGE 8: John Muir's desk and papers in the Martinez home, now protected by the National Park Service as a national monument. 200mm lens with available light; High Speed Ektachrome.

PAGE 25: The second Muir farm, near Montello, Wisconsin. Built by the Muirs after they moved from Fountain Lake, the farm has been owned by only two other families since the 1850s. The people in this shot are the father and son of the present owner. 28mm lens; Kodachrome II.

PAGE 26: The windmill on the second Muir farm. Young John almost died digging this well under orders from his father. 20mm lens; Kodachrome II.

PAGE 27: Fountain Lake. Originally part of the first Muir farm, the lake is now surrounded by a county park. 20mm lens; Kodachrome II.

PAGES 28–29: A gathering storm over cornfields near the Muir farm. 28mm lens; 1/30 second exposure; Kodachrome II.

PAGES 30–31: A sheep flock and shepherd in the San Joaquin Valley near Fresno, California. Muir grew to hate domestic sheep during his summers as a sheepherder, referring to them as "hooved locusts." The sheep pictured here are grazing on a harvested cornfield that has been rented to the rancher. They will stay until they have devoured all the stubble and will then be moved to another field. SHEEP: 20mm lens; Kodachrome II. SHEPHERD: 200mm lens; Kodachrome II.

PAGE 32: Thunderhead over Yosemite Valley. 200mm lens; Kodachrome II.

PAGE 49: Sunset light on El Capitan Rock, Yosemite Valley. 28mm lens; Kodachrome II.

PAGES 50–51: The view east from Glacier Point across Half Dome toward the High Sierra. Glacier Point is 7,214 feet; the top of Half Dome, 8,842. Several of the peaks in the background are over 12,000 feet. 20mm lens; Kodachrome II.

PAGE 52: Glacier polish on granite near Tuolumne Meadows. It was glacial evidence like this that caused Muir to venture farther into the Sierra until he discovered the glaciers themselves. 20mm lens; Kodachrome II.

PAGE 53: Exfoliating granite in the Yosemite high country. 200mm lens; Kodachrome II.

PAGES 54–55: Tuolumne Meadows at sunset. 20mm lens; Kodachrome II.

PAGE 56: The top of Nevada Fall at sunset. I had set three tripods on the bridge across the fall and was waiting for the best light when I glanced over and saw a large brown bear ambling toward the bridge. I waved and screamed to scare him away, but he kept coming. When he reached the bridge, he stopped and gave me a look that could be roughly translated as, "Beat it!" I tried to explain how long it had taken me

to set up all the equipment; he wasn't interested. I asked if he might consider waiting till the sun set; he started across. What would Muir have done in a situation like this? I asked myself. But before my mind could answer, I was already beating a hasty retreat, cameras and tripods in hand. 28mm lens; Kodachrome II.

PAGE 57: Hikers on the Mist Trail beside Vernal Fall in Yosemite Valley. 200mm lens; Kodachrome II.

PAGES 58–59: An early fall storm breaks to reveal the walls of Yosemite Valley covered with snow. 200mm lens; Kodachrome II.

PAGE 60: A thin skin of ice on a high-country pond foreshadows the arrival of autumn. 50mm Micro-Nikkor lens; Kodachrome II.

PAGE 61: Dying daisies in Yosemite Valley. 105mm lens; Kodachrome II.

PAGES 62–63: Tuolumne Meadows in late fall. The boulder in the foreground is an erratic deposited here by a glacier. 20mm lens; Kodachrome II.

PAGE 64: Upper Yosemite Fall, which plunges 1,430 feet, is probably the highest leaping waterfall in the world. A torrent in the spring, it slows to no more than a trickle by fall. 400mm lens; High Speed Ektachrome.

PAGE 81: "Smoke" Blanchard, head of the Palisade School of Mountaineering, makes a tricky move while climbing on the east side of the Sierra near Bishop, California. 20mm lens; Kodachrome II.

PAGES 82–83: Mount Whitney at sunrise, taken from a light plane. This peak, at 14,495 feet, is the highest point in the United States outside Alaska. 28mm lens; Kodachrome II.

PAGE 83: A climber approaching the summit of Cathedral Peak, Yosemite. (What some photographers won't do to get the right camera angle!) The first ascent was made by John Muir. 20mm lens; Kodachrome II.

PAGE 84: A breaking storm over Banner Peak (12,945 feet) in the eastern Sierra. 28mm lens; Kodachrome II.

PAGE 85: Mustang clover blossom in Sequoia

National Park. 55mm Micro-Nikkor lens; Kodachrome II.

PAGES 86–87: Mount Rainier, near Seattle, Washington. Muir was one of the first fifty persons to climb to its summit. 20mm lens; Kodachrome II.

PAGE 88: Indian paintbrush on the slopes of Mount Rainier. I needed a person in the picture to complete the composition, and I hadn't passed anyone on the trail for hours, so the man in this shot is me. 28mm lens; Kodachrome II.

PAGE 89: Fireweed and cow parsnip in Gustavus, Alaska, near the entrance to Glacier Bay National Monument. I had gone out that morning to fly over the glaciers at sunrise, but my ride to the plane never showed up. At first, I was furious and sat by the side of the road totally oblivious to the beauty around me. Luckily, my anger passed, and as I looked around, I realized that the pictures I should be taking were right in front of me. How often one will miss a good shot by deciding what *should* be happening rather than what *is*. 200mm lens; one second exposure at *f*22; Kodachrome II.

PAGES 90–91: A brown bear fishing for salmon on Ann-Ann Creek near Wrangell, Alaska. 400mm lens; High Speed Ektachrome.

PAGE 92: Another beached iceberg in Glacier Bay. 20mm lens; Kodachrome II.

PAGE 93: For six thousand years this patch of ground was covered by a glacier. It had retreated only six short years before this picture was made, and these fireweeds were the first new plants attempting to grow there. As summer at Glacier Bay is relatively mild and the elevation low, they are probably succeeding. Some areas that lay buried under glaciers in Muir's time are now dense alder forests. 20mm lens; Kodachrome II.

PAGES 94–95: The Plateau Glacier in Glacier Bay National Monument. In the four years since this picture was taken, I am told, this glacier has completely disappeared. 20mm lens; Kodachrome II.

PAGE 96: A fishing boat searching for salmon near Wrangell, Alaska. 200mm lens; Koda-

chrome II.

PAGE 137: A baby woodpecker peers from his nest in Sequoia National Park. The mother had built the nest in an old stump only a few feet from the ground. I put my macro lens just inches from the nest and waited until curiosity overcame one of the babies. 55mm Micro-Nikkor lens; Kodachrome II.

PAGES 138–139: Giant sequoias in Sequoia National Park. At one time these great trees were being dynamited to make grape stakes for wine growers in other parts of the state. 20mm lens; Kodachrome II.

PAGE 140: A Belding ground squirrel in Tuolumne Meadows. 200mm lens; Kodachrome II.

PAGES 140–141: Shelf fungus, Yosemite Valley. 55mm Micro-Nikkor lens; Kodachrome II.

PAGES 142–143: Sunset on Half Dome, Yosemite. In 1872, Muir noted in his journal: "About four o'clock in the afternoon, the valley grows dim like a half-lighted room. You may see no cloud nor well-marked shadows, but cold thin twilight gathers, nevertheless. You judge it must be sundown, and look west down the valley for the sunset, but it is not visible, nor can you see any sky on which a sunset might be. Then, turning to look up the valley to the eastward, you discover your missing sunset on Half Dome." 20mm lens; Kodachrome II.

PAGE 144: A polished piece of petrified wood. 55mm Micro-Nikkor lens; Kodachrome II.

PAGE 145: Petrified stumps in Petrified Forest National Park. Before the park was formed, these stumps were to be ground up into sandpaper! 20mm lens; Kodachrome II.

PAGES 146–147: The Grand Pacific Glacier, Glacier Bay. 28mm lens; Kodachrome II.

PAGES 148–149: Waterwheel Falls, Yosemite, by moonlight. 20mm lens; 1½ minute exposure; High Speed Ektachrome.

PAGES 150–151: View from Moro Rock, Sequoia National Park. 200mm lens; Kodachrome II.

PAGE 152: Jeffrey pine on Sentinel Dome, Yosemite. 20mm lens; Kodachrome II.

Index

(Page numbers in italic type indicate illustrations.)